Sleep Little Baby, No More Night Tears

You Don't Need to Look Like a Zombie. Discover Every Steps of The Proven No-Cry Solution and Feel Rested, Energized and Ready to Take Over

Table of Contents

Introduction 5

Chapter 1 - The Basics of Baby Sleep 10
    Baby Sleep Cycles By Age 10
    How Do Sleep Cycles Differ By Age? 13
    5 Fascinating Facts About Your Baby's Sleep 17
    Important Precautions To Keep Your Baby Safe As They Sleep. 19
    What About Co-sleeping? 21
    What About You? How To Manage On Broken Sleep 22

Chapter 2 - Getting Organized 26
    Everything You Need for Your Baby's Sleeping Area 26
    Where Should Your Baby Sleep? 29
    Sleep Associations: What They Are & How They Can Help 29
    What is a Sleep Log? 36

Chapter 3 - Baby Sleep Problems 38
    8 Common Baby Sleep Problems by Age & How to Manage Them
    38
    Fixing Less Common Reasons for Poor Sleep 42
    What Your Baby's Sleep Habits Mean 46

Chapter 4 - Preparing for Sleep Training 49
    Hard Truths about Sleep Training that All Parents Must Know ... 50
    Is Your Baby Ready for Sleep Training? 54
    How to Choose the Right Sleep Training Method for Your Baby 57

Chapter 5 - Sleep Training Success 60

4 Transformative Sleep Training Methods 60
Sleep Training in More Detail: Here's How 64
How to Make Sure Your Baby Sleeps Through the Night 66
Why Sleep Training Fails & What to Do 68

Chapter 6 - It's Naptime! 71
Strategies for a Successful Naptime 72
What if Your Baby Won't Nap? 75

Chapter 7 - No Problem Too Big 77
Understanding Sleep Regressions by Age 77
How to Deal With Sleep Regressions 80
6 Must-Know Sleep Strategies for Single Parents 82
Two Babies, Many Solutions 85

Chapter 8 - Completing Your No-Cry Toolkit 90
How to Soothe a Crying Baby 90
Baby Crying Patterns by Age 92
5 Effective Remedies for Colic 93
Helping a Sick Baby Get Restful Sleep 96

Conclusion **101**

Introduction

Lack of sleep is one of the things many parents find most unbearable when they come home with a new baby. And for a certain amount of time, it's simply part and parcel of being a new parent. But there are things you can do to make your baby sleep better, and this book will give you all the information you need to enjoy more peaceful nights with your baby or toddler.

By the end of it, you should feel ready to make the right choices for your family about sleep training, along with setting up a daily routine, handling naps and illness, and dealing with a crying baby. I have tried here to distil both everything I have learned from raising two babies, and everything that the parenting experts know about babies, toddlers and sleep.

Sleep training isn't always easy, and it can lead to a few upset nights. A crying baby is hard for any parent, and if you've picked up this book because you have tried and failed to get your baby to sleep, you have my sympathy. Learning to fall asleep, and stay asleep is something that comes more naturally to some babies. But for others, unfortunately, it takes time and effort on the part of often exhausted parents to support their baby to sleep deeply and wake up refreshed and happy.

Add in curveballs such as colic and common childhood illnesses, plus parents dealing with more than one baby, or single parenthood, and it's no wonder new parents are struggling.

If this is you, you're no doubt exhausted and wondering what to do next – should you try sleep training, controlled crying, or some other technique you haven't read about yet? Are you doing something wrong? Is there something wrong with your baby? What is the secret of those mothers who have such 'good' babies; those who sleep through the night without complaint?

Rest assured, it is completely normal to ask all of these questions throughout your parenting journey. But please know that sleep problems are also totally normal with babies and toddlers, and over time things will improve. Babies simply need to adjust to the world they've arrived in, and some find this easier than others. This doesn't make them 'good' or 'bad' babies – it just makes each of them unique! Sleep problems in the early years are simply part of being a parent, and don't mean you are doing anything wrong. Sometimes, working around the poor sleep and finding ways to cope is your best option, and I will show you how to do that in the chapters to follow, along with safe and gentle sleep training options.

If you are due to have your first baby soon and want to get ahead with your parenting skills, this book will also be very useful and make those early days a little easier.

The best training is on-the-job, and as a mother who has raised two babies, I have been through the early, sleep-deprived days of living with a new baby, and know what worked for me. It may not be exactly what works for your baby – that is for you to discover. What is easy for one baby may not be easy at all for another, which is why it can be frustrating to receive so many different pieces of advice from well-meaning outsiders who don't know your baby as well as you do. Your instincts about what your baby needs are always worth listening to. Let them guide you as you find your way, and remember, even if people sound like they know so much more than you, everyone who parents is mostly winging it.

I don't try to offer my readers a perfect one-size-fits-all solution (which, when it comes to parenting, doesn't exist anyway). What I offer to you instead is a range of strategies to try, all based on sound research and the latest findings around baby sleep. All are based on both looking after my own babies and doing my own extensive research and reading around baby sleep. As someone who looks back on those sleep-deprived early days with mixed feelings, I always think of things I could have done better. Personally, with my first baby, I let the broken nights go on for far too long. With my second, I was more confident about taking charge, and he was a better sleeper from an earlier age.

Read on to discover all of the different things you can try to get your baby to sleep better. When you try these approaches, you can look forward to a less fretful and exhausted baby who will be far more engaged and happy in his or her waking hours. The other, very important, benefit will be for you – with more sleep and less time trying to get your baby to sleep, you'll feel so much better, have more energy and be able to get on with the business of living alongside your baby.

As with anything to do with your baby, it's always worth getting an expert opinion if there's anything that's bothering you. Help is out there, and you only have to ask. But for many parents, it's simply a matter of knowing what to expect and how you can guide your baby in the right direction.

I will also cover in detail all of the things you need to think about in relation to safe sleep – the equipment you need, where your baby should sleep, and how to avoid any accidents. We'll cover strange sleeping habits, how to keep a sleep log and how to carry out sleep training, should you feel it's what you need for your own and your family's well being. Nap times, sleep regression, and getting your baby to sleep well when she is sick are other areas you may find helpful at particular times on your journey. And we'll look at sleep issues for single parents, as well as those looking after more than one baby.

What I offer are not clear solutions, but a framework and guidelines for you to try, to see what works for you. When it comes to babies and toddlers, this is the only sane approach! Rest assured that by establishing routines and a gentle timetable around sleep, as well as some consistency, you will be well on your way to better nights.

So settle back, and work through this book in your own time, taking note of what works for your baby, leaving behind what doesn't, and may trying things a little further on down the track – sometimes your baby just needs a little more time.

I promise that by the end of it, you'll have many new ideas to work with, and will be starting to see the light at the end of the tunnel. What I don't want you to do is fall into despair about your baby's sleep – these precious months when your baby is small will pass quickly, and ideally there should be many moments of joy for you, too.

Let me assure you again that there are many ways in which you can help your baby become a better, longer sleeper. Please know that when this happens, your daily life together will become so much easier. It's also worth remembering that not all problems can be solved by you, but by the passing of time – your baby will grow up a little, learn new skills, and suddenly what was bothering you about their sleep has simply stopped happening. This is one of the most amazing things about parenting – watching as your child grows up, develops, learns new skills and becomes their own person. Each stage brings its own rewards along with the questions.

As well as helping your baby adjust to the world, you also have to take charge constantly as a parent, always noting what works for your particular baby. Sleep is one of the key areas you will need to focus on and feel confident about as you start your new life with your baby. And as a parent, acting with consistency and confidence is often the key to success.

Here is a guide to help you do just that.

Chapter 1 - The Basics of Baby Sleep

In this section, we'll touch on baby sleep cycles by age, so you can understand your baby's sleeping habits better. Babies change so quickly at this stage of life as their brains and bodies grow rapidly. Having a basic understanding of what to expect from your baby's sleep at each stage, and what you'll need to wait a little longer for, can be both helpful and reassuring to new parents.

Like everything else they have to master, babies need to **learn** how to sleep at night and stay awake during the day – it isn't something they can do from day one. It's also helpful to know that the wakefulness and unsettled sleep of a tiny newborn is partly a survival mechanism to keep them from falling too deeply asleep when they need to feed regularly and their lungs are still so new. Better sleep does come with time, and this is something all parents need to accept to some extent. What you can do, though, is understand what to expect at each stage, and in later chapters we'll look at how to nudge your baby in the direction of good sleep habits.

In this chapter we'll also give you five fascinating facts about your baby's sleep. And finally, we'll cover the all-important precautions you can take when setting up your baby's sleeping area to keep him or her safe during naps and night time sleeping.

Ready? Let's get started.

Baby Sleep Cycles By Age

As a rough guide to work with, here's how much sleep babies and toddlers will need over a 24-hour period, varying between naps and longer sleeps at night.

Newborns: 16 hours, though it can be as little as eight and as much as 18

Three-month-old babies: around 15 hours

Two years plus: around 12 hours

Of course, as with everything, these times can vary between individual babies, and you'll quickly gain a sense of your own baby's sleep patterns. You'll also soon learn to value their sleep and do whatever you can to protect it, as it results in a much happier, more contented baby in their waking hours. And not only will a well-rested baby be more enjoyable and easy to be around, regular, deep sleep is essential for their growth and development.

One of the biggest shocks I received when I brought my first baby home from the hospital was when I tried to put him to bed on that first, exhausted night. *That was all pretty intense*, I thought to myself, *but at least now we can all have a good night's sleep and see where we are in the morning.*

For some reason, I simply assumed that because we were home, life would return to normal. He would understand that it was late and we were going to sleep now, right?

Of course, it didn't work out that way. The minute I turned off the light, my baby was wide awake and screaming for two hours solid as I tried to feed him, soothe him, comfort him – and get him back to sleep. Many unsettled nights followed, and it took me a while to get that full night's sleep I was expecting, but eventually, sleep and sanity returned. Sorting out feeding problems helped a lot, but much of it was due to him being so new to the world and unsettled by everything and everyone around him.

What I also soon realised from talking to my midwives and my own research was that newborns have no sense of night or day. To some extent, their sleep patterns are governed by their mother when they are in the womb, and the rise and fall of her own activity and hormone levels. But once they are born, their mother's movements no longer dictate their sleeping and waking times, and they need to establish their own sleep habits in time with the outside world.

You may notice that your baby seems particularly alert at night, which is totally normal for newborns. This will generally start to get better at around six weeks old, which is when the intensity of the newborn phase – the screaming, colicky hours and the unsettled behaviour – will often start to ease a little generally. It can be helpful to think of the first three months as a 'fourth trimester' when your baby is still adjusting to life outside the womb, and keep your environment as peaceful as you can, particularly if you have an unsettled, nervous baby (if you do, you'll know what this means.)

Having said all that, you may also wonder if there are there any ways of speeding up this process of getting newborns into a normal day-night sleep cycle? Yes! There's lots you can do. Playing with your baby and taking him outside in the daytime, and creating a quiet, dim, even boring, environment at night, will help him to learn that night is for sleeping. As adults, our sleep is governed by circadian rhythms – we feel alert during the hours of daylight, especially if we go outside and expose ourselves to natural light soon after waking, and at night time, when the lights begin to dim, our bodies produce melatonin, which readies us for sleep.

Your baby will soon do the same, but in the meantime, it's best to simply allow for the broken sleep, let other people take care of you, don't try and do too much or worry about "getting into a routine." For now, as much as you can, simply enjoy the precious newborn bubble. You can and will sleep later, I promise!

How Do Sleep Cycles Differ By Age?

Adult sleep cycles consist of deep 'soundless' sleep and REM or active sleep, which is also the dreaming phase of sleep and essential for healthy brain function, as it's when your brain essentially puts all its files in order. During REM sleep, the body is temporarily paralysed, but brain activity is noticeable, with irregular breathing and eye movements. An adult sleep cycle will last about 90 minutes, and at the end of it we either wake up or start a new cycle. Baby's sleep cycles are slightly different, and it helps to be aware of this.

Newborns (birth to three months)

A newborn will cycle between quiet and active sleep, and each cycle is shorter than an adult sleep cycle at about an hour long, up until around nine months of age. Unlike adults, babies will **begin** with active sleep, which is similar to REM in adults, and are more likely to wake up in this stage, particularly if they jerk and startle themselves. Around half of their sleep is spent in 'active sleep', compared to only 20 per cent for adults. While babies are asleep, their movements during this sleep may mean that the adult assumes they are waking up. But often, if they are left alone at this point, they will continue to sleep.

This need to be 'held together' to fall into a deep sleep is why many babies respond well to firm swaddling, up until the age of about two months.

Around halfway through the sleep cycle, the baby will settle into a quiet sleep, with slower breathing, stillness and no eyelid fluttering. This is the end of the sleep cycle, after which the baby will either awaken, or begin a new cycle of active sleep. You will soon start to recognise the quiet sleep, which is less unsettled. However, very small babies tend not to have periods of long, deep sleep as older babies do.

By three months of age, rather than starting in REM or active sleep, babies will start a sleep cycle in deep sleep, like adults, which can make it easier for them to fall and stay asleep.

You'll find that once your baby starts onto solid food, around six months, their sleep will improve even more, and once they start moving independently they will tire themselves out more and sleep even better.

Newborns will tend to sleep off and on throughout the day, and while you can't control this completely, you can work around it and gently guide them towards sleeping at night and being awake during the day, with a couple of naps in between.

Newborns are also often quite light sleepers and will spend about half their time in active, not deep sleep. Because they are so small, their bellies can't hold much food so they will wake regularly to feed – as they grow, they will wake less often and will eventually 'sleep through' until (early) morning.

You'll also notice that a "good sleeper" won't necessarily stay that way. Newborns may start off sleeping very deeply and regularly, but at around three weeks they will start to become less settled — sleeping less and crying more, often for no apparent reason. Around this time you may see one longer sleep of up to five or six hours, a couple of three hour sleeps, several two hour sleeps and five or six hours of drowsing, crying, and catnapping. No wonder parents of newborns are exhausted from all that broken sleep!

Infants (three to 11 months)

By three months, your baby may have settled into a regular routine, with a morning and afternoon sleep and sometimes an extra one, too. The morning sleep tends to be quite long, with one or two afternoon naps to follow before bedtime.

You can expect your baby to sleep for around 14-15 hours a day, with some babies sleeping for up to eight hours at night.

The active sleep phase is reduced, and they will start to sleep more deeply. You can expect them to wake at least once at night, with some babies waking every three hours for a feed.

At around six months, the total amount of sleep a baby has per 24 hour cycle will reduce to about 13 hours a day in total. The naps will also reduce – many babies drop the morning nap first (a sad day, but it also means you can go out more easily in the mornings!), but continue to have one or two afternoon sleeps. However, many children will continue having an after-lunch nap well into toddlerhood.

At around six months of age, babies will also begin to move towards a more typical sleep cycle, with longer cycles and less time in active sleep. Gradually, over time, they will build up to sleeping for a solid eight to 12 hours of uninterrupted sleep.

Babies at this age will also usually sleep better at night, though some may wake up and need to be settled back to sleep, often with a feed. Separation anxiety, which appears at this age, can also cause some babies to feel more clingy and wake in the night for reassurance, particularly if they have been separated from you during the day.

Establishing daytime and bedtime routines and creating a flexible structure can help your baby to get to sleep at night. We will cover all of this in detail in the chapters that follow.

Toddlers (12 to 36 months)

Around 12 months, your baby will start to move into toddlerhood. With this increased maturity, and more movement and activity in their daily life, they will be sleeping better at night and only wake up once or perhaps twice at night.

By the time they are around two, they will need approximately 12 hours' sleep over a 24-hour period, although they may have longer sleeps during growth spurts and developmental leaps – if this happens, work around it, as they really do need as much sleep as they can get at this age, when their brains are growing so quickly. We will cover the sleep regression that sometimes comes with growth spurts in later chapters. Sometimes, I would notice my toddler having an especially long, deep sleep, and waking up with a new skill that I hadn't seen before – it was as if the extra sleep had actually been an intense training session for a developmental leap.

5 Fascinating Facts About Your Baby's Sleep

1. The more they sleep, the more they sleep

An overtired, fretful baby can find it difficult to get to sleep, then find it hard to enjoy being awake, creating a cycle of bad sleeping. But good sleep creates more of the same. So keeping a baby awake when they are tired, to try and make them sleep better at night, will actually have the opposite effect. It seems counterintuitive, but a wired, overtired baby will find it harder to get to sleep than one who is put to bed earlier. Prioritising your baby's daytime sleep and getting into a regular routine is the best way of working towards better nights, and this is what we will focus on throughout this book.

2. Morning light promotes good sleep

Taking in natural light in the daytime, and creating a dimly lit environment at night, will stimulate the production of melatonin, a hormone that promotes sleep. This works for adults as well as babies – going outside and getting some natural light on your face soon after you wake up can be helpful if you suffer from insomnia as it 'sets' your body clock. Be sure to get outside with your baby – for a walk around the park, to the shops, or just out in your back garden – every day, so that they start to set their body clocks as quickly as possible. As we'll cover in later chapters, the variety and stimulation babies get from being outside is also an essential and easy aid to encourage better sleeping at night.

3. Babies take longer to reach a deep sleep – around 20 minutes.

Because babies start off in active, not deep sleep, they can move and grimace a lot in their sleep. So even if your baby seems unsettled, leaving them in peace will often result in them reaching deep sleep eventually. If you can, try to resist rushing in to soothe or pick them up when they first fall down – they may seem upset, but in fact they are busy falling asleep, or very close to it. If you find this difficult, force yourself to go and have a five-minute shower. You won't be able to hear any crying, you'll get five minutes to yourself, and you may just come out and find that your baby has fallen asleep in your absence.

4. Night waking are essential to their survival.

While it can be frustrating being woken through the night, your baby needs to wake up to fill their tiny belly. Once they are a little bigger, their sleep cycles will lengthen and you won't have such broken nights. They also may wake up suddenly due to a startle reflex and getting them back to sleep can be difficult. As mentioned earlier, some parents find that swaddling their baby in a soft blanket or sheet can hold them still and help them settle and stay asleep for longer. Swaddling is easy and often helps with broken sleep – look online for videos of how to swaddle a baby.

5. Babies learn as they sleep.

During REM sleep, research shows that blood flow to the baby's brain increases, as their brains work hard to integrate all the new information they have been given that day. Sleep is essential to brain development, so the more you can learn about sleep techniques and help your baby to achieve them, the better. During REM sleep you may notice your baby twitch, breath irregularly and move their eyes. They stay in REM sleep for about half of each cycle, which may be because at this age, they have so much learning to do. For this reason, too, you should avoid waking a sleeping baby as much as possible (as if you would!).

Important Precautions To Keep Your Baby Safe As They Sleep

To keep your baby safe as they sleep, here are some essential guidelines to follow. We will cover some of the points in more detail in the following chapters.

- Always put babies to sleep on their backs, both at night and when they have daytime naps. Once they are a little older, they may find their own position as they move around throughout the night, but always put them to bed on their back.

- Sleeping should be done only on a firm surface, such as a mattress in a safety-approved crib or bassinet. Avoid soft fluffy blankets or cushions.

- It's recommended that you share a room with your baby for the first six months. A cot attached to your bed, with an open side that can be dropped down for feeds, is a solution that will ensure everyone gets enough sleep. Babies often sleep better if they know their parent is in the room, although once you attempt sleep training you will need to move your baby (or yourself) into another room, at least temporarily – more on this later.

- Use a fitted sheet and keep all soft objects, toys, padding and pillows away from the sleeping area. A zip-up sleeping bag with a fitted neck and armholes is a safe option for sleep as it can't cover the baby's face. These sleeping bags come in different thicknesses so you can choose the right one for your climate and time of year. They also serve as a useful sleep cue, telling your baby it's time to go to bed – again, more on sleep cues later.

- Never smoke around your baby, or allow other people to smoke in areas where your baby spends time. If someone has been smoking, they shouldn't hold a small baby. Smoking is associated with an increased risk of SIDS, so keep your environment completely smoke-free, and avoid it when you are out, too, especially if your baby was sick or premature at birth.

- Never fall asleep with your baby on a sofa or other area apart from the safe sleeping area. If you want to sleep close to your baby, set up an open cot next to you bed so the baby is close but safely out of the way. Planning co-sleeping like this is far safer than accidental co-sleeping, particularly when everyone is exhausted and can fall asleep very deeply.

- Never sleep near your baby if you have been drinking alcohol or are otherwise under the influence of drugs, or particularly exhausted. And never allow others who are under the influence of drugs or alcohol to fall asleep near your baby either. Pets should not share a sleeping area with babies, either.

- Keep an eye on the temperature of the room and ensure that it remains comfortable – not too hot or too cold. Keep your baby's head uncovered, and dress them in the same amount of clothing you would wear to bed. Overheated babies are at an increased risk of SIDS.

- Ensure everyone looking after the baby, or living in the house, is aware of safe sleeping practices, too. And finally, babies should never be left alone to sleep in cars, or in car seats, or unsupervised in prams.

What About Co-sleeping?

Some parents choose to co-sleep with their babies, and find that it works very well. Others don't choose to co-sleep but find instead that it chooses them, as their baby will not settle anywhere else but close to them at night. If you do choose to co-sleep, ensure that you are doing so safely. Sharing a bed is not safe if the baby is sharing a bed with a smoker, or if there are adult blankets that may cover the baby, or if the parent is drunk, drugged, obese or very tired.

If you do choose to co-sleep, ensure that your mattress is very firm, and that the baby cannot fall off the bed (a mattress on the floor is the safest option.) Put the baby on one side of the bed, not between two adults, dressed in a sleeping bag, not covered in adult blankets, and ensure that everyone knows the baby is in the bed.

You should also be aware that the risk of Sudden Infant Death while co-sleeping is most common in the first eleven weeks. Personally, at this age, I had my babies in a cot next to my bed, with one side removed, so there was no chance of me rolling onto them, but they were close by. Once they were older, they sometimes ended up next to me in bed, but for the most part they were in their own safe space. As with everything, it's always worth talking to your doctor and child health nurse before making a decision that works for you and your family. As mentioned earlier, accidental or unplanned co-sleeping, when you fall asleep with your baby unintentionally, is more dangerous than planned co-sleeping.

So now you know the basics of baby sleep from birth to toddlerhood, and know what you can expect in terms of sleep quality and length at each age. You also know how to set up a safe sleeping area for your baby. Let's move on to ways you can encourage deep, refreshing sleep for your baby so that he or she thrives and is happier in the daytime. But first, let's look at how to manage as a new parent on broken sleep.

What About You? How To Manage On Broken Sleep

Now that we've established that you won't be getting a full eight hours' sleep a night for some time, let's have a quick look at how you can help yourself through these early days. This time will pass, and you will sleep again, but it's important to go easy on yourself and not feel like you have to be your normal, well-rested self. Personally, I found the broken sleep and tiredness to be the hardest part of being a new parent. I couldn't hold proper conversations, I felt flat and exhausted a lot of the time, and I couldn't seem to think clearly or plan for the future. In retrospect, I wish I'd gone a bit easier on myself – napped more, gone to bed earlier, and not worried so much about the future and "getting everything under control." If you find you are really struggling, always seek help early from your doctor, in particular if you find you can't sleep yourself, even at night time.

Some baby experts refer to the first three months after the baby's birth as a Fourth Trimester. By this, they mean it's a time when you are still very much in the pregnancy and birth bubble, and should be resting and nesting much as you did towards the end of your pregnancy.

It's also a time when your baby is adjusting to life outside the womb, and you're getting to know your new baby and learning to be his parent and read his signals. Let's now look at some ways to make what can be a rough and intense time easier for you. This, in turn, will make it easier for your baby.

Tips to help you get through the early days on broken sleep.

- Mark your calendar for three months after the birth, and allow yourself, in that time, to take it easy, rest and focus on simply feeding your baby and yourself, and getting as much sleep as you can. Of course you won't be able to do this all the time. And you may feel thrilled that your pregnancy is over and ready to be out and about much sooner, especially if your baby turns out to be a good sleeper. But at least allow yourself to take it a bit easier in that first intense newborn stage – particularly if you don't have a great deal of family support around you, as many of us don't.

- Prepare ahead with some frozen meals, and perhaps get a regular online shopping order set up. Hire a cleaner, if your budget allows, or some extra help around the house, such as a post-natal nurse or night nurse. Allow others to help if they offer, with offers of food or just holding the baby so you can get a rest or a shower.

- Limit your obligations and don't feel bad for saying no to visitors, particularly those demanding ones who expect to be waited on while they hold the baby. It's natural for everyone around you to be excited about a new baby, and want to spend as much time as possible cuddling and holding the new addition. But keep visits short if you don't feel up to it, and if your baby doesn't like being handed around for hours (many find it stressful and it can lead to an unsettled night) then simply take your baby and retreat to your bedroom. There is plenty of time for everyone to get to know your baby in the months and years ahead, and you have to prioritise your own well-being, and that of your newborn, at this special time.

- Sleep when the baby sleeps. Hard to do, when it feels like the only time you have 'off', but try not to stay awake if you could be sleeping, whenever possible. In the evenings, having a warm bath and some skin-to-skin with your baby and then an hour or two of sleep. This will make a big difference to how you feel the next morning. Especially if it ends up being an unsettled night!

- Agree on a timetable with your partner about who does night time wake ups. If you fall asleep early, perhaps your partner can do the first wake-up feed of the night, so you will get a good four or five hours of sleep before the next one – express a bottle of milk if you are breastfeeding, or have him wake and bring the baby to you, then settle him outside of the bedroom so you can fall straight back to sleep. Sharing the broken sleep means that the burden isn't just on one person.

- Prioritise eating well. When you are exhausted it can be easy to fall into the habit of existing on toast and coffee. But you will need nutritious food to recover from the birth, and to keep your energy levels high. Have some cut-up fruit and vegetables close to hand, enjoy soup, yogurt, salad and other easy meals. Drink lots of water, and try and get some protein and healthy carbohydrates into your diet, too. Keep taking your pre-natal vitamins as you rest and recover from the birth, and don't drink too much coffee, as it can interfere with your sleep.

- Finally, remember that time spent with your baby is the most important thing right now, as she settles into the world and your bond grows. Give yourself lots of time to settle her. Ask visitors to make their own drinks rather than waiting on them hand and foot. And put your feet up as much as you can. You've just been through a huge physical and emotional life change, and you need to treat yourself accordingly!

Chapter 2 - Getting Organized

We now know what babies and toddlers should be doing when it comes to sleep. We know that newborns are naturally unsettled, and that there are things we can do to help them along as they learn how to sleep properly, such as getting some natural light in the daytime. And we know how to set up a safe sleeping area for the baby.

What we also need to understand is that there's no magic trick to create a perfect sleeper – sometimes you just get lucky, other times you have a fretful baby who struggles to fall and stay asleep. What you can do is educate yourself about how to encourage good sleep.

In this chapter we'll build on this knowledge and dive into how we can establish the right environment for good sleep. We'll learn about sleep associations, and how they can help your baby to get ready to drift off. And we'll also look at creating a sleep log, which can help you develop a better understanding of how your baby's sleep is changing over time. This can be helpful both for your own peace-of-mind, and also to show your GP or child health nurse, should you decide to seek further help with your baby's sleeping habits.

Everything You Need for Your Baby's Sleeping Area

- Sheets: Around six cot or bassinet sheets is perfect, and you can also use folded single-bed sheets if you need to. You can also put a pillowcase over a small mattress when your baby is very little.
- A mattress protector to put over the mattress will protect it from leaking bottles and nappies. Or use a blanket or a towel underneath the sheet.

- A mosquito net may be helpful in the warmer months, if you live in a mosquito-prone area. There is nothing worse than waking up to a miserable baby covered in mosquito bites.
- A cot or bassinet. A small bassinet is great for the first few months, but you can also put your baby in a cot from the start. Ideally you want something that's easy to move, and that allows you to access your baby easily, for example during night feeds and if you need to pat your baby to sleep.

Some cots come with two levels, so you can raise them when the baby is small then lower them once your baby is old enough to climb out of the cot.

When choosing a cot, look for smooth, rounded edges and no extra decorations such as beads, which can be hazardous. The cot should have high sides so your baby can't fall out once they are a bit older (ie two feet from the base of the mattress to the top of the cot sides). If it has drop-sides, they need to be childproof and work smoothly, and the mattress should fit the cot well. Your cot also needs to have no more than two to three inches between bars, so your baby can't fit his or her head through.

If you are buying a second-hand or vintage cot, be aware that old paint may contain lead. You'll need to strip or repaint the cot, if this is the case. Also ensure that any decorations on an old cot can't be pulled off, and that the cot is strong and sturdy.

- Babies tend to settle and sleep better on a dense, firm mattress, so look for these when you are shopping around. A good-quality clean, firm, second-hand mattress is fine – just leave it in the sun for a day or two to air it out.

- Cot bumpers (a soft piece of padded fabric that surrounds the inside of the cot) are no longer recommended by baby safety experts, as they can restrict air flow to the cot and also pose risks of suffocation or strangulation, should they come loose. There should be absolutely no extra fabric, pillows or soft toys around a sleeping baby. Children do not need pillows until they move into a toddler bed.

Do you need any additional safety products?

There is no substitute for planning your baby's sleeping environment and following the latest safety guidelines, remaining vigilant and using your common sense and instincts when it comes to keeping your baby safe while sleeping.

Having said that, a night light can be very helpful to cope with night feeds, and so you can move around without waking the baby too much. It can also be a comfort to your baby once they are older and wake in the middle of the night.

A sound monitor can be used if your baby's nap area is a long way away from your living room for day time naps. If your baby sleeps in your room for the first six month, you won't need it for night time – you'll hear him! However, sleep monitors don't monitor breathing, so can't be considered a safety device, and one downside is that they can be disruptive, as you will hear every noise your baby makes while sleeping.

Breathing monitors may be given to small or unwell babies, but are not generally used for all babies. They have an alarm that goes off if the baby stops breathing, but can also give frequent false alarms. I always recommend that all parents should know how to do heart-lung resuscitation, though, so you know what to do in an emergency.

Where Should Your Baby Sleep?

Ideally, for the first six months, your baby should sleep in your room for safety reasons. If, after this point, you decide you would like the baby in a separate room, the risk of SIDS (Sudden Infant Death Syndrome) drops, but it is still safer to have the baby in your room for the first six months, and as long as you like into the future. Refer to the first chapter for information about co-sleeping safely, or consider having a cot next to your bed so you can hear and reach your baby easily.

Sleep Associations: What They Are & How They Can Help

Sleep associations are essentially signals that make your baby feel sleepy. As adults, we develop them too – reading in bed before sleep, a warm bath, a particular time each night that we head for bed, and our pre-bed rituals such as brushing our teeth and putting on our pyjamas.

Setting up sleep associations for babies is much the same thing, and as your baby grows and you settle into living with him or her, you'll find a routine around sleep will help you to organise your days better and enjoy a well-rested, happy baby.

Read on for some ways you can create sleep associations and start to establish a routine with your baby.

Create a flexible daily routine

Strangely enough, your day time routine is itself a powerful sleep association. Research shows that if your baby is part of your daily routine, he or she will develop mature circadian rhythms more quickly, and thus sleep better at night. In other words, take your baby with you on your daily activities so you are active and quiet at the same times. Studies on infants have shown that regular exposure to daylight will help your baby adapt to the cycle of day and night. It's also been shown that babies exposed to light in the afternoon will sleep better.

A daily routine may look something like this:

- Wake up. Give your baby a feed, then get dressed and head outside, weather permitting, to the playground or shops so you have some daylight and fresh air. Some 'play' in the form of eye contact, singing and chatting to your baby will also stimulate them and ready them for a good sleep later on. Activities such as baby swimming lessons or a children's session at a local library are other ways to fill your morning.

  Tummy time is great for giving your baby some exercise and strengthening his neck and shoulders, and can be done on a soft rug from birth. Some babies love it, others hate it, but if you build up gradually to around 15 minutes a day it's a great first workout for your baby and will help to tire him out. Tummy time should always be done under supervision – hold a toy in front of your baby's face to keep them happy as they work out.

- Home for a morning nap
  With a very young baby, this will be only an hour or two after waking. For older babies and toddlers, it might be after lunch. You will know your baby is tired as they will start to complain and perhaps cry, avoid eye contact, and start to rub their eyes

or clench their fists. Each baby has their own 'tired' signs, and you will soon start to recognise yours.

- Wake up
  Now it's time for lunch, play time, and try to get outside for a walk and some more daylight. Board books, singing, movement and chatter are other good ways to give your baby the stimulation she needs to learn and grow.

- Afternoon nap
  With very young babies, there is not much point trying to predict nap times as they aren't established straight away, and will change from day to day at first. But older babies will start to fall asleep reliably in the afternoon for a longer nap. Ideally, they should be awake again by three, or four at the latest, if you want them to be in bed again for 7.30pm, but this is up to the individual baby.

Some babies can be up at five and asleep again by six; others will be up until 10pm if they are asleep past four pm. You will need to track your own babies sleep to work out when and how much sleep they need – we will cover sleep logs in a later chapter.

- Evening routine and bedtime
  Creating a predictable bedtime routine is key to establishing good sleep habits and making sleep training run more smoothly later on. Start with dinner, or a feed, followed by a warm bath, perhaps a massage, and then quiet time before bed with lots of cuddles, singing, a top-up feed and maybe a board book or two,

then lights out at the same time each evening. Busy days with lots of attention, chatter and cuddles for your baby will "fill their cup" so they are more ready for sleep at night, too.

Please note that you don't have to live by this routine – depending on your own nature, you might prefer more flexibility. But with babies, a flexible, yet predictable routine can provide structure and security for your little one, and help you feel more in control, too.

Create a strong sense of night time being sleep time

Helping your baby understand that night time is for sleeping is crucial for establishing a good sleep routine. At night, after dinner, a warm bath can help to make your baby ready for sleep. Doing the same things before bed each night – a story, some quiet time in their sleeping room – will also ready them for sleep.

Throughout the night, too, make sure that wake times are as quiet and boring as possible to convey to you baby that *there's nothing happening here, it's time to sleep.* Minimise eye contact, and don't have any play or bright lights or screens on during night feeds or wakings (this another reason a night light can be useful).

Try not to move your baby too much if you are feeding them, as this will help them to stay drowsy. An open-sided cot bed next to yours will help you deal with night wakings with as little disruption as possible. If you need a light to see what you're doing, choose a very low wattage so the room remains as dark as possible. Black-out blinds on the windows can also help to keep your baby from waking too much during the night.

Introduce wind-down time at night, and try to stick to it

Even if you aren't following a strict routine, it's a good idea to give your baby plenty of time to wind down at night. Think of your own night time routine and how it's easier to get to sleep if you've carried out familiar rituals beforehand, such as putting on your night clothes, and brushing your teeth and maybe reading a book. Your baby will respond to sleep cues, too – it's just a matter of finding ones that work for you. These could include the following:

- A warm bath, perhaps with some lavender oil added.
- A massage in a warm, dimly lit room, with soothing oils. A bedtime massage has been shown to improve baby sleep.
- A bedtime story or two – simple board books will do. It's not so much the 'reading' but the cuddling in bed, the calming reading voice, and the familiarity of the ritual that will settle your baby.
- Skin to skin contact for very small babies, who may like to be tucked up against you in bed to fall asleep.
- A bedtime song such as Twinkle Twinkle Little Star.
- A soft, soothing stroke of the back or hand, although not all babies will like this and it may actually wake some up – you'll need to test it yourself!
- Feeding your baby right before sleep, then putting them down and waiting until they drop off, is also a way to help them fall easily into sleep.
- Feeding your baby to sleep is also an option chosen by many mothers, including me. Eventually you need to break the association with feeding and sleep, but when the time is right, it will happen. We will get to that later!
- If you don't want to get into the habit of feeding your baby to sleep, you can feed her until she is drowsy, perhaps already

dressed in her sleeping bag, then settle her in her cot so that she drops off on her own, knowing you are close by but not 'needing' you to fall asleep. This will teach her that she can put herself to sleep, and may make things easier in the long run. As with everything, though, you will need to work out what your particular baby prefers and go along with that, to some extent. More highly strung or clingy babies may resist being put down in their cot to sleep and will only fall asleep in your arms – there's nothing wrong with this, particularly in the early days, so don't let anyone tell you you're "creating a rod for your own back" – everything can be changed when the time is right.

Ensure the temperature is right

An overheated room isn't great for sleep quality or for safety. Body temperature changes throughout the day, and once we fall asleep it naturally drops. Ensuring your baby's body temperature drops off at bedtime will encourage a deeper sleep, and can also help them fall asleep faster. If the temperature is too hot or cold, the baby's body will try to regulate it, and it will take longer for sleep to descend.

The ideal temperature is between 68 and 72 degrees Fahrenheit (or 19 to 21 degrees Celsius.) If it's hard for you to achieve this in your house, dressing the baby suitably is the next best option. As I have already mentioned, sleeping bags that your baby wears are the safest and most reliable option for good sleep – you can buy them in varying tog thicknesses to suit your particular climate and time of year. Generally, go for a thick tog in winter, a thin one in summer, and dress your baby in a sleepsuit underneath that covers his or her feet. You will soon work out what's best for your baby, and if they are overdressed they will look red and fretful, and feel hot to the touch. If your baby's chest or belly feel sweaty, remove a layer of clothing or dial down the heating.

The right temperature is also essential for safety. The risk of Sudden Infant Death Syndrome, or SIDS, increases in winter when babies might be bundled up under too many blankets and overheat.

Create darkness

As with all people, babies cycle between periods of wakefulness and rest, but unlike adults, they have no way of controlling this for themselves. When they get overstimulated and tired, they need to transition into an environment of low stimulation so they can fall asleep. One of the best ways of doing this is to create a room that is very dark. This is easy at night, and in the daytime you can achieve it with a blackout blind that can be placed over your window with plastic suction cups. As soon as your baby sees the dark room they will begin to anticipate sleep, their muscles will relax, and they will begin to feel drowsy. And indeed at any time of day when your baby gets upset or overstimulated, taking them to a quiet, dim room will help to calm them down.

Minimise noise and use white noise, if necessary

As with bright light, too much noise can be overwhelming for babies, who will become overstimulated and find it even harder to drop off. Obviously you can't create a perfectly soundless environment, but you can use white noise within your baby's sleeping area to block out other sounds.

White noise can reduce stress, encourage deeper sleep, and reduce any overstimulation. You can buy white noise generating machines, or use an app on your smartphone. It's important, though, that the white noise isn't too loud (no more than 50 to 60 decibels), or too close to the crib. And while it can be helpful for some babies, it may not work for all of them. But it's worth a try! If you want to phase it out eventually, you can just dial it down a little each day until it's off.

A table or ceiling fan is another sleep aid that can be helpful, both for the monotonous sound and for the air movement, which can promote a restful sleep.

What is a Sleep Log?

Some parents like to track their baby's sleep on a sleep log. This can be as simple as a notebook, or you can use an Excel spreadsheet or even an app to record your baby's sleep. Logging the length and timing of your baby's night sleeps and naps may help you identify a pattern to their sleep, and keep track of just how many hours of rest they are getting. This may be useful to show your child health nurse, or to simply get a better understanding of your child's need for sleep.

You will also be able to note changes over a longer period of time, and perhaps get some comfort from the fact that your baby's sleep is gradually improving. And a sleep log may also help you work out just how much sleep your baby needs to be happy and alert during the daytime, if you look back a day or two and note just how much sleep they have (or haven't) had, and compare it with their behaviour.

Sometimes, paying attention to their sleep can solve certain problems. For example, my son would go to bed at night easily as long as he was awake from his afternoon nap by no later than 3pm. Any later than that, and he would be up until 10pm. So I would always aim to have him down for his nap by 1.30pm, and around 3pm I would start gently making a little noise and allowing him to wake up. Once you work out how your child's sleep works best, you can plan around your 'best practice' findings accordingly.

While a sleep log won't work for everyone, it's useful to keep track of your baby's sleeping patterns, and will help you feel more in control, too. There are even shareable online apps that you can use to log naps and other information, which you can share with other caregivers looking after your child.

Chapter 3 - Baby Sleep Problems

8 Common Baby Sleep Problems by Age & How to Manage Them

Newborns and small babies

At this age, you have to accept a degree of disrupted sleep. It will pass, but my best advice is to give yourself a break. As I've said earlier, take all the help you are offered, don't give yourself a hard time about a messy house or a takeaway dinner, and know that it will soon be over and everyone will be sleeping better. Just rest, enjoy your newborn and recover from the birth and pregnancy. It's honestly not for long. Having said that, there are a few sleep issues you may come up against that you may want to address for safety reasons or just because they will make your life easier and aren't difficult to fix.

- Not being able to sleep on their back

At this age, it's recommended that babies are always put to bed on their backs, as any other position increases the risk of SIDS. One solution is to swaddle babies firmly in a blanket to help them feel more secure and stop them flailing around. Another is to rock them gently to sleep, then move them into their bassinet or cot once they are deeply asleep. If you are consistent, she will eventually get used to sleeping on her back.

- Not knowing the difference between night and day

As we have discussed, babies have no sense of night or day, and wake frequently throughout the night to feed. We've looked at ways you can start to give them a sense of night and day, which will help over time.

These include going outside and getting some natural light in the daytime, and keeping nighttime wakings as dark and quiet as you can, so she gets the message that darkness is for sleeping.

- Hunger

If you are breastfeeding, be sure to keep in touch with a lactation consultant to ensure that your baby is getting a good feed, as a hungry baby will find it hard to sleep. Breastfeeding can take a while to establish, so in those early days you may need to hold your baby or feed for a long time to get them off to sleep. Always get as much help as you need and you can look forward to better sleep once the feeding routine is established.

With bottle-fed babies, again, ensure that the baby is getting enough food, checking the instructions for mixing the formula up carefully. A warm bath, followed by a feed, should ensure a good sleep.

Two to three month old babies

- Sleep regression

Around this age your baby should be sleeping better, however you may also notice a sleep regression. This often accompanies a growth spurt or development leap, and is characterised by an alert, active baby who shows no signs of wanting to sleep. There's not much you can do apart from work on solidifying your night time routine – bath, story, bed – so that your baby gets the message that nights are for sleeping, not playing. It will soon pass, but if it's exhausting you, see if you can get some extra rest or naps in the meantime. We will look more at sleep regressions later on.

Feeding through the night is another habit you can fall in to, especially with breastfed babies. Your baby feeds little and often, leaving you exhausted. If you keep your baby in your room with you, you may be able to manage night feeds without fully waking up. But if you would like to stretch out the time between feeds so you get more sleep, try and give your baby a really good feed last thing at night, and perhaps express a bottle of milk so your partner can take over one feed (although this may be more hassle than it's worth, and some breastfed babies will simply refuse a bottle and hold out for the breast. Creating set times for bottles or breastfeeds in the daytime and trying to stick to them may also guide your baby towards a more regular sleeping and feeding pattern through the might.

- Teething pain

Some babies may seem unsettled when they have a tooth coming through, with red cheeks and drooling. Extra cuddles, a teething ring and a warm bath will all help to settle him. Teething will generally pass quickly, but if your baby seems to be particularly unhappy, a visit to your family doctor is worth a try, as they may recommend some baby painkillers which will help with sleep, too. Having said that, teething can also be used as a catch-all term for any unsettled behaviour – sometimes, it's worth looking a little deeper to find out if there's any other solutions to usettled behaviour.

Four to five month old babies

- Overstimulation

Around this age your baby may drop a nap, and start sleeping less in the daytime. This may lead to her being overtired at night and harder to settle. It's important to realise that an overtired baby may 'fire up' and become much more active, loud and energetic, rather than sleepy.

This can be a sign of overstimulation, so if your baby seems overtired, try starting the bedtime routine a little earlier with all its associated sleep cues so they can catch up on sleep.

My second son used to "flap" himself to sleep, discharging extra energy by pumping his arms up and down. Even now, at six, he will do a bit of gymnastics before bed. It doesn't mean he isn't ready for bed, though, so I will firmly guide him to his bed at the right time and he will fall asleep within minutes. Babies and children often fight sleep – but don't let them win!

Sometimes, with an overtired baby, it takes longer for them to wind down, which can create a vicious circle of another late night followed by another unsettled day. It may help to 'break the cycle' with a busy afternoon that includes some play and outside time, followed by a good feed, a long bath and an early bedtime. No matter how alert your baby seems, keep in mind ideal sleep quantities for each age bracket and aim to get them – very tired children won't learn and thrive as well as well-rested ones.

Six months

- Still waking up wanting a feed

Although we don't remember it in the morning, we all wake up during the night a couple of times, and fall back to sleep again almost immediately with no memory of the event. Babies need to learn to fall back to sleep as well, preferably on their own and without requiring too much help from their caregivers, past the age of about six months.

If you've been feeding your baby to sleep, you might now consider moving this feed to thirty minutes before bedtime, and following it with a board book story and some lullabies in bed. You can expect some fussing at this change of routine, but if you are consistent, she will drift off without the bottle or breast if she is tired. This will hopefully also make night wakings easier – if she learns that she can get back to sleep without a feed, just your voice and perhaps a gentle stroke should be enough to settle her again.

Of course, if you don't mind feeding through the night, don't feel you have to do this. But if you are exhausted during the day, it might be a good idea to introduce some gentle sleep training around six months to make day-to-day life easier. There will be much more on this later!

- Early waking

Some babies wake early, raring to go. You can try adjusting naps and bedtimes, or put a black-out blind over the window to try and push her wake up time back a little. Another option is to bring her into your bed and hope that she drifts back to sleep.

Ultimately, though, early mornings are part and parcel of having a young baby, so getting to bed earlier yourself so you can handle the early start may be the best solution.

Fixing Less Common Reasons for Poor Sleep

Sickness

Unfortunately sickness – an upset tummy, an earache, a cold – can all result in terrible sleep. Keep on hand a baby painkiller recommended by your doctor or child health nurse so you can administer it when pain strikes in the middle of the night. Hopefully, the illness will pass quickly and sleep will return. But when this happens, you may have to simply accept a disrupted night and hope for some respite the following day. We will cover more on handling sleep problems caused by sickness later on.

Travel or a change of routine

Even now that my kids are older, I accept that the first night in a new place is going to be difficult. A change of routine, the excitement of a new environment and possibly a long nap on the journey will all result in a bad night's sleep, or a late, drawn-out bedtime. However, by the second night, everyone should be exhausted and sleep well.

Travel with babies can be difficult for this and many other reasons, so my suggestion is to manage your expectations and take things easy. Travelling with children does get easier as they get older, and more fun, particularly once everyone can read and swim. But in the early days, it's not always relaxing or even worth the hassle, a lot of the time.

At these times, if you have some kind of a routine or structure that is familiar to your baby – such as a warm bath, followed by stories in bed – you can always return to this to give your child the signal that it's time to sleep. Extra cuddles and lots of reassurance will also help.

At times of disruption – travel, growth spurts, developmental leaps – a familiar routine is a great way to keep things on track until everyone adjusts to the new reality.

A new caregiver or starting daycare are other things that can cause your baby to be unsettled and fussy, often just when you need them to be 'good.' Remember, your baby isn't trying to make your life harder, they are just unsettled and need you to show them that everything is fine.

Personally, I have always been a huge fan of stories in bed with my babies and young children. It is a nice way to unwind together at the end of the day, and as your child grows it will help them with talking and learning about the world and using their imagination. Plus, reading to your children will set them up very well for school later on – any time you give it now will pay off later.

Only sleeping while being held

This is a tricky one, and some trial-and-error is required if you want to break this habit. Often, introducing a white noise CD while rocking or holding your baby will give her another sleep cue. After a few days, you can try putting her down while playing the white noise, gently patting, rocking or shushing until she is asleep.

Sometimes babies need to know you are there to fall asleep. So if you are trying this, stay with your baby until he is deeply asleep. Shush, pat, rock – do anything apart from lie down with your baby or pick him up. He may object, but will soon learn that he can fall asleep without being held, as long as he knows you are there. Once he has taught himself to drift off, you will be able to leave the room earlier without too much trouble.

An overtired baby that finds it hard to get to sleep

If you get to know your baby's signs of tiredness – rubbing eyes, grizzling, sometimes clenched fists – you will know to put them down at the first sign, if you can, before they get really exhausted and overtired. Sometimes, though, you miss that magic moment and it becomes harder to get your baby to sleep as they are so worked up. Sometimes, a pram or a car drive can help as the movement lulls them to sleep. Or staying with them in a dark room until they drop off is another way to break through the overtiredness and allow sleep to arrive.

Only catnapping for short periods of time

Some babies will only sleep for twenty minutes then wake up again, still seeming tired. In this case, go back to basics and look at your whole sleep routine and environment. Is the room dark, quiet and the right temperature? Are you putting her down soon enough? Putting a baby down to sleep when they are already overtired can make it harder for them to reach a deep sleep. Also, look at your nighttime routine – are you following a set pattern each night, with afternoon play and daylight, a good feed, long bath and set bedtime? Putting in place a firmer structure can help some babies adjust and sleep better. Sometimes, though, it's just a matter of getting through until they learn to sleep better, and if this is the case, you may need to look at ways to cope with less sleep, which we looked at earlier one.

Falling asleep in the car or the pram

With some babies, they may fall asleep while you are out, and you'll find that when you get home and attempt to put them into bed, they wake up again, missing their nap. If this happens to you, it may be easier to not disturb them once they are asleep. If they are in a pram, simply wheel it somewhere quiet and keep an eye on it until they wake up. If you are in a car, park somewhere shady and pull out a book or your smartphone, keeping the air-conditioning or heating on depending on the weather. If you take snacks and drinks with you when you are out, you can simply enjoy nap time in your car. But never, ever leave a sleeping baby in a car unattended.

What Your Baby's Sleep Habits Mean

If your baby finds it hard to fall asleep

They may be overtired or unsettled for some reason. In this case, it's often good to start bedtime earlier, and see if that helps. An overtired baby will find it much harder to get to sleep.

They may be hungry. Around six months, when your baby starts eating solids, they may suddenly start to sleep much more deeply. You can also try introducing high-fat, dense foods to satisfy their hunger. Toast with lots of avocado and butter, for example, is a dense, high-fat food that will fill your baby up. Another good food is pureed chicken soup – the protein is very filling.

They may be having a growth spurt or developmental leap, or unsettled for some other reason. More on this later.

Unexplained unsettled behaviour

Unfortunately, there is never a 'one size fits all' solution when it comes to baby behaviour. Nor is there a set of guidelines that will solve all of your sleep problems. What you can do is understand what is normal behaviour and also keep in mind that the tricky phases will pass with time. Sometimes, just ensuring you get enough downtime by cutting back on other activities if you are feeling worn out is the best solution. Whatever your baby is struggling with usually won't last for long, and as time goes by your sleep will return.

Other strange sleep habits

Snorting and snoring

Babies make all sorts of funny noises, and snorting or snoring during sleep is nothing to be concerned about. Babies may also snore gently when they have a blocked nose. A vaporiser or humidifier in the room, or sitting with your baby in a steamy bathroom, may help to clear their nasal passages and make them more comfortable before sleep. Having said that, a baby who snores all the time, not just when under-the-weather, is worth seeing your doctor about, as it may be a sign of a health problem. Your doctor may refer you to a paediatric ear, nose and throat specialist for further tests.

Heavy sweating during sleep

Some babies tend to 'run hot', and you will notice that they sweat a lot while sleeping, particularly during their deep sleep and sometimes soaking their sheets. Because babies spend 50 per cent of their sleep time in deep sleep, if they sweat during this time, it will tend to be more noticeable. Always check the temperature of the room and ensure your baby is not overdressed, as overheating can be a risk factor for SIDS.

You should also mention excessive sweating to your doctor, as it can be a sign of an underlying health issue. Don't feel you have to pile your baby with blankets – they will let you know if they are cold, and you can also check how warm they are by feeling their hands or chest.

Of course, babies can also simply get very hot in summer. If you're hot, your baby probably is too. A warm, but not hot, bath and perhaps a clean wet flannel to suck on in the bath can ensure your baby stays cool and hydrated enough to drift off to sleep. But if the house feels cool and your baby is not overdressed yet still feels very hot, talk to your doctor.

Rocking and headbanging

Babies may sometimes get on all fours and rock in bed. It looks strange, but it's totally normal, particularly when they are drifting off to sleep. Babies also sometimes practise new physical movements while half asleep, again and again, until they finally lie down and sleep. Keep an eye on your baby if they are doing this in bed – it's quite fascinating! – but don't worry too much. It may be accompanied by head banging or rolling – again, weird, but totally normal. This often happens around six to nine months, when babies start to master new skills around movement and crawling.

Head banging may also be a distraction from the pain of a tooth coming in, and can continue for some time. It's rarely a sign of anything serious, but it's worth mentioning it to your doctor, especially if your child is showing any other signs of developmental delay.

Teeth grinding

Many babies grind their teeth, especially during sleep. It's also common when the first tooth comes through. It sounds awful, but isn't anything to worry about. You can, however, mention it when you take your baby to her first dental appointment, at around one year of age.

Chapter 4 - Preparing for Sleep Training

Sleep training is something that you might want to consider when you and your baby are both ready, if you feel desperate for sleep and want your baby to learn to drift off to sleep on her own. While it doesn't work for all babies (or parents), I believe that it's a reasonable approach that can have a positive impact on family life. Yes, there might be a few days of crying and broken sleep, but an exhausted parent who is waking every few hours to pat, rock and feed a baby is not ideal in the long-term, either, particularly if it's affecting your mental health, happiness levels, work and relationships.

Bear in mind, though, that you don't have to sleep train if you don't want to. If you can live with broken sleep, and find ways to manage, such as co-sleeping or napping when your baby naps, you don't need to do anything. It's up to you, and you should always do what feels right.

If you don't want to sleep train, simply continue with your bedtime routine and other strategies for night waking we have already outlined, and work around it until your baby is sleeping better, or you decide that the time is right for sleep training. You might choose to keep the baby's cot next to your bed, or place a mattress in the baby's room, or alternate 'on duty' nights with your partner until your baby is better at getting through the night without waking.

Ultimately, as with everything to do with looking after a baby, you can look at the research and current information, take what you can and decide what will work for you and your family. Before we dive into the nitty-gritty of sleep training, though, we need to look at what it is. We'll also cover how to work out if your baby is ready for sleep training, and how to choose the right sleep training method for your baby.

Hard Truths about Sleep Training that All Parents Must Know

Sleep training, sometimes (wrongly) referred to as 'crying it out', is essentially teaching your baby how to fall asleep on their own, or with limited help.

You can go in to the room periodically to provide reassurance – patting, stroking and soothing – but you don't pick the baby up or take him into your bed. The aim is to 'train' your baby to fall asleep independently, without all the rocking, cuddling, bottles, breastfeeding and other sleep aids you have been using.

It can be a divisive issue. Some people believe that you should never leave a baby to cry, that you will do untold psychological damage, and that you should simply go along with what the baby wants. Child development experts don't always agree on whether it's an appropriate solution to poor sleep. But what we do know is that it's possible to introduce some sleep training in a gentle way, without simply closing the door on your baby and leaving them alone until morning. In the old days that was known as the 'crying it out' method, and we have definitely moved on from that! Here are some things you need to consider when deciding to sleep train.

Sleep training doesn't always work

Whether you follow the old-fashioned (and no longer recommended) path of leaving your baby alone until morning, or try a more gentle approach, be aware that success is not guaranteed. Both methods work with some babies, but not all of them. Some will put up more of a fight, and you may have to accept this and remind yourself that in a few years they will be in their own beds and sleeping well. And that when they are teenagers you will struggle to stop them from sleeping at all, and you will perhaps long for their baby days!

Bear in mind, too, that for around 20 per cent of babies, sleep training simply doesn't work – they may be too young, or not able to cope with separation from their parents. Like so many parenting scenarios, it comes down to your child's unique temperament. And yours, too – you may find that you can't cope with the sound of your baby screaming for you in distress, and abandon the idea on the very first night.

It's not something you need to beat yourself up about

Some parents find it incredibly hard to make the decision to sleep train, worrying that they are being cruel or causing their baby long-lasting emotional damage. What you need to keep in mind, though, is that in the setting of a loving, safe family environment, sleep training is unlikely to do any lasting damage. And in fact, if you are returning to work, looking after other children or driving regularly, it's essential for you to get a good nights' sleep too, for safety reasons and for your own mental health and wellbeing. So please don't beat yourself up about wanting to change your baby's sleep habits. Sometimes, for the good of the wider family, it's worth at least trying.

Bear in mind, too, that once upon a time, parents had much more family support to draw on, with grandparents and other family members stepping up to help with childcare and quietly appear in the small hours to give exhausted parents a break. Plus, these days, many women combine work with childcare, so need to be alert and busy during the day.

Today's families also tend to be much smaller and more contained, and nearby family help or help from older siblings is not always available. What this means is that problems with sleep fall squarely on the parents' shoulders (often the mother's). It's not unreasonable, in today's pressured parenting environment, to work towards a good night's sleep!

It's a good idea to address sleeping problems sooner rather than later

With babies and children, the longer you leave a particular behaviour unaddressed – whether that be thumb sucking or falling asleep in front of the TV – the harder it is to eventually change it. So if you lie down with your baby every night, or feed them to sleep, they will get used to it and not want to change. If you don't mind, it's fine – you don't need to change anything. But if you want to spend less time at night on bedtimes, for example, you're better off addressing it head on rather than waiting and hoping that things will change by themselves. Chances are, if the baby likes it (and if it means being close to you, they will) they won't change without a bit of a struggle. There will be some pain and crying while you put in place the new habits, but if you are firm, consistent and determined, the pain will be short lived and you can look forward to everyone having better sleep and your evenings back. As a parent, you are in charge, and if you are consistent, your child will come to the party eventually. They want to please you, after all.

There is no set formula that is guaranteed to work

Some sleep training books will offer a very structured approach to sleep training, but what you need to remember is that the authors don't know your or your baby. So what works for some babies won't work for others – and it doesn't mean you're doing anything wrong. What you need to look for is what some researchers call the 'magic moment' when your baby will stop crying and gradually drift off to sleep. This may be due to lots of reassurance and visits from parents, or your baby may do better if you remove yourself from the room for a little longer between visits.

You will work this out yourself, and you may be surprised to discover that your baby needs a bit of time to do some 'unwinding' crying on their own, knowing you are nearby, in order to get to sleep.

Even now, my pre-schooler son will often fall asleep faster if I leave him alone, even though he may call for me. If I go in, he wants to chat and engage with me, and the whole process takes longer. Eventually, you will work out what helps your particular baby. You'll also be able to tell the difference between a falling-asleep, not particularly distressed cry that is simply the baby unwinding and releasing pent-up stress before sleep, and a seriously distressed, anxious cry that is not going to result in sleep any time soon.

It's important to remember, too, that some crying in babies, toddlers, children and even adults is healthy. A good cry relaxes us and discharges emotions and tensions, so don't feel that you are doing your child any harm if they are left to cry a little. Sometimes, it's simply part of their falling-asleep process, and helps them to relax and wind down. It's only a problem if you leave them to cry alone for hours, or ignore any serious distress. A calm, relaxed approach, with some gentle words of support, is the best way to handle sleep training.

What you definitely don't want to do is to try sleep training, abandon it, then try again, on and off for an indefinite period of time. This is unfair on your baby, as they don't know what you want from them and they won't know what to expect from bedtimes.

Your baby may sleep better after training, but there will still be bad nights

Sleep training isn't a miracle solution, and it's not about solving all of your baby's sleep problems for ever. It's more about improving matters so that ideally your baby can drift off to sleep independently, and you feel more rested in general.

You will still have nights when your baby needs you – perhaps they had a bad day, feel unwell, or they are going through a growth spurt or developmental leap and need some extra reassurance. There's no harm in going to your baby in the night when they cry out for you – that is simply part of being a parent. It doesn't mean you need to pick her up or bring her into your bed, though, unless you want to. Once you've done some basic sleep training, your baby should generally be able to get back to sleep with a few gentle words and a reassuring stroke from you. And if you have an unsettled night due to sickness or some other reason, return to your routine as soon as possible so you don't undo all the progress you've made.

In summary, it's up to you – and in the context of a loving home, many child health experts believe that some gentle sleep training is worth a try if you are feeling exhausted and irritable.

Is Your Baby Ready for Sleep Training?

Around six months is a good time to think about whether your baby is ready for sleep training. Before this time, it's developmentally appropriate for your baby to be waking in the night for a feed, and they can't really be 'trained' to sleep for longer. But if you decide you want to try and change things, don't wait for too long after this point, and sleep habits will be more established and harder to break.

By six months of age, a baby will be used to you picking them up and rocking them back to sleep, and perhaps feeding them, too. But if you feel you would like more sleep, then there is nothing wrong with trying to change things a little. So if at this point you decide you would like to try sleep training, it may be that over a period of three or four nights of some crying, you will find that your baby is settling and sleeping much better.

So when is sleep training recommended? Read on for some common reasons to try sleep training.

If your baby is waking through the night to be fed.

Here, you may not mind feeding your baby through the night. There's nothing wrong with doing so, particularly if you are breastfeeding and your baby is close by, and you can feed without either of you waking up too much. But if you are still waking through the night to heat bottles and your baby requires soothing and rocking to get back to sleep, it's not unreasonable to at least try to change things at this point.

Around six months is a good time to try this – your baby is likely to be much more settled and relaxed, and you have gotten past the initial shock of a new baby. If you feel you'd like to push for a bit more routine around sleep, give it a go.

If your baby is unable to drift off to sleep alone

Again, this may not be a problem for you. But if you have other children to look after, or you simply want your evenings back and would like your baby to be able to fall asleep independently, trying some gentle sleep training may be a good idea. Single parents and parents of twins may also need to try sleep training sooner for practical reasons.

As your baby gets bigger, rocking to sleep can become harder, so you may find that your aching arms make the decision for you! The end result will ideally be that you carry out your usual bedtime routine, as we discussed in earlier chapters, settle your baby in bed, and he or she falls asleep independently, perhaps with a little 'wind-down' crying. And you get your evenings back!

If your baby is sleeping longer at night already

Once your baby is bigger, and eating three meals a day, and sleeping well at night, you may consider sleep training to move your baby into better long-term sleep habits. If waking up to breastfeed or have a bottle in the middle of the night is no longer necessary from a nutritional point of view, but seems more like a habit, you may choose to train now.

If your baby shows some ability to self soothe

If your baby seems relaxed in general, and falls asleep easily without seeming fretful or distressed, you may want to try sleep training now. Some babies are temperamentally more highly strung than others, but if you feel like your baby will respond well to sleep training, and you are generally happy with her development, there's no harm in giving it a go at six months of age. You can always try again at nine or twelve months if it doesn't work. If you're really lucky, you might end up with a baby who prefers to drift off to sleep without any extra attention. Though if that's the case, you probably won't be reading this book!

The timing is right for your family

Addressing disrupted nights and trying to get your whole family sleeping better is going to take a few nights of disruption, effort and willpower on your behalf. Factor this in, read up on sleep training, and plan your approach and time so that you have the best chance of success. Don't sleep train when you are busy at work or with other activities and need your rest. Make sure you don't have other things on, such as visitors coming to stay or a holiday away from your home and routine. Nor should you attempt to sleep train when your baby is sick or otherwise unsettled with some new change in his routine, such as starting at a new daycare.

Choose a time when everyone is well and happy, and you can give it your full focus for a few nights. If it doesn't work, so be it. You can always try again in a few months time.

How to Choose the Right Sleep Training Method for Your Baby

There is no one sleep training method that is guaranteed to work. Research shows that they all achieve around the same degree of success, but it will depend on what works best for your child and his particular temperament. The most important thing is to be consistent. The four main methods are "Cry it Out", "Fade Out", "Pick up Put Down" and "Camping Out."

And there's the final method, that you may find, eventually, is that the best thing for you and your family is to co-sleep with your baby, because he or she demands to be close – up to you. You can always try sleep training again later.

As I've mentioned, by the time your baby is around six months old, you'll have some idea of his temperament. In fact, you'll get a sense of his personality as soon as you meet him, but by six months you should know whether he's a fretful, clingy baby or a more relaxed one. Does he need to be close at all times or is he happy for periods alone? Is he determined to always have his own way, or does he show some flexibility? All of these factors will help you decide what kind of sleep training to use.

The first thing to work out is if you need to sleep train at all. If you are lucky, you may have a baby that can naturally self-soothe. Try this test: put your tired, well-fed baby to sleep and let him cry for a little while. He may drop off to sleep quickly all by himself, in which case you don't need to sleep train at all – lucky you!

But it's not always so easy. Generally speaking, a very sensitive, highly strung child will need a slower approach, or may not cope with sleep training at all.

A more strong-willed child may need a firmer approach, and be left to fall asleep largely on his own with a few nights of crying, because a parent coming into the room will strengthen his resolve to fight back against the new system!

Other, relatively easy-going babies often respond well to more gentle "No Cry", "Fading Out", or modified cry-it-out methods.

You also need to think about your own temperament: do you have the resolve for a fast, cry it out sleep training programme over a short period of time, or do you feel more comfortable taking longer to sleep train, but doing it more gently? Sleep training can be particularly hard when you are already sleep deprived, and for any parent, the sound of a crying baby is quite unbearable.

Plus, you need to think about other people in the family. Will children be woken by late-night screaming? Do you have a partner who can help share the burden of sleep training? You are looking at a minimum of three nights of disruption, with many babies taking seven to 10 nights before they are fully on board. So plan your strategy accordingly.

Ready to dive in?

In the next chapter, we'll give you a range of sleep training methods to try, from gentle training to faster methods that you carry out over several nights. We'll also look at what you need to do to succeed, and what happens if it doesn't work.

Chapter 5 - Sleep Training Success

4 Transformative Sleep Training Methods

Before we dive into the various sleep training methods, it's important to understand that there are no guarantees. And, as with everything to do with babies, there is no one answer. What you may end up using is a combination of the methods described below. You may find, once you start, that even two minutes of crying is unbearable for you, and choose to opt for a more gentle method. Always follow your own instincts here, and never do anything that makes you feel bad. But also try not to feel guilty about a bit of crying. It honestly won't do your baby any permanent damage. Permanent harm to children comes from things like abuse, war, food shortages and homelessness. So remember to keep the issue of sleep training in perspective!

It's developmentally normal for babies to cry before sleep – it helps them to discharge stress and tire themselves out, and you are not a 'bad parent' if you decide to try and get more sleep or help them fall asleep on their own. Remind yourself of the overall benefits of everyone getting more sleep, and also that famous parenting manta, "This too shall pass." An exhausted parent is not good for her baby either, and if you are returning to work or have other commitments, such as other children, it's perfectly reasonable to try and get your baby into better sleep habits.

Before you start, remember to implement a semi-regular day routine, with enough interesting and varied activity that your baby is left tired but not completely exhausted. Try and incorporate a walk or outing, some daylight, some 'play', a visit to a new house or relative, and lots of chatter and singing, etc, as well as three healthy and filling meals.

Naps should be regular and ideally not too late, as if your baby is overtired he will find it harder to settle.

This busy day can be followed by a set sequence of pre-bed rituals, as mentioned earier – a warm bath, perhaps a massage with some lavender-infused baby oil, a board-book story or two, a lullaby, lots of cuddles, and zipping your baby into his sleepsuit. Keep the lights low, turn the TV off, and make sure there is nothing interesting happening in another room that your baby will pick up on and want to investigate!

All of these rituals will send the message to your baby that it's time to relax and sleep, and make sleep training run more smoothly. If you have been feeding your baby to sleep, you can try breaking this association by feeding before stories and sleepsuit, rather than at the end. Keep calm yourself throughout the bedtime ritual, even if you are desperate to get the baby to sleep so you can have some time to yourself. Your baby will always pick up on your mood, so if you seem agitated or impatient, it may take longer to get him drowsy and drifting off.

Essentially, get your daytime house in order, including daytime naps and a bedtime ritual, before you try and tackle nights. We will cover naps more in an upcoming chapter.

OK – let's now move on to the four most common sleep training methods, and the benefits of each.

Fading out method

This has a number of names, but I'm calling it the Fading Method here. Essentially, with this method, you put your baby down to sleep after his normal bedtime ritual, and leave the room. At this point your baby will usually cry for you, but rather than go in immediately, you wait for a minute or so, before going back in to soothe, reassure and say a few gentle words. But you do not pick up your baby.

Gradually, you increase the amount of time you are out of the room, stretching it by a minute or two, until you are out of the room for 10-15 minute at a time. Ideally, your baby tires himself out and drifts off to sleep. If this method is going to work, it should do so within a week. Some people find that this method distresses the baby more, as every time you reappear in the room you upset the baby once again. Others find that it works well and after a few days to a week their baby is falling asleep with minimal crying and distress.

This is the standard method that works best for most parents, so it's the one that I cover in detail later on. Other methods are simply variations of this one – some more gentle, one more dramatic. But this is the one I strongly recommend you start off with, and then adapt depending on your baby's response.

Cry it out method

Also ominously knowns as the Extinction Method, this is the classic method that most people think of when they hear the words 'sleep training.' It may also be called 'controlled crying.' This is essentially putting your baby to bed and not returning for a long period of time, sometimes even until morning. It's hard on the baby, who may become very distressed, and it can be hard on parents too. Generally, I think it's better to accept that you are going to have a few nights of disrupted sleep attending to your baby and hopefully they will sleep better at the end of it. Most parents would find it very difficult to fall asleep to a screaming baby, anyway.

Pick up Put Down Method

This method is similar to the Fading Out method, in that you go in and out of the room for gradually lengthening periods of time. It differs, though, in that instead of reassuring your baby with words and strokes, you pick him up to soothe him, before placing him back in his cot. For some babies, this extra holding makes them feel secure and they will eventually drift off to sleep. For others, though, being picked up and put down will over time make them overstimulated and distressed, and they will fight sleep harder.

It can also depend on how you are feeling – if you find yourself getting agitated and upset by your baby's crying, he may pick up on that and become more distressed himself.

This method is, however, quite gentle, so you can start it with babies who are just a couple of months old. It may work from a very early age, and if it doesn't, you can simply try again a little later.

Camping out method

This involves being in the room, sitting on a chair, to offer reassurance, but not picking up your baby, rocking them, or feeding them. Gradually you move the chair further and further away until you are out of the room. The baby knows you are there, but gradually learns to fall asleep on her own.

This method can be used when others have failed, but can be distressing for parents if your child becomes very upset and you feel that you 'shouldn't' pick him up. However, it does mean you don't have to leave your baby alone to cry, which some parents find unbearable.

Another option here is to set up a pull out mattress next to your baby's cot, so they know you are there but can't really see you or engage with you. You can take the time to have a rest while they drift off to sleep (or bring in your smartphone, as long as your baby isn't distracted by it) and then simply tiptoe out once they are asleep. However, you may question how successful this is as your baby is still using your presence as a 'sleep aid'. It's not easy!

Sleep Training in More Detail: Here's How

I will now cover the Fade Out sleep training method, which you can adapt based on how your baby responds. This gives you a basic method to follow, but is in no way prescriptive – you'll have to adapt it to suit your temperament as well as your baby's. This is the one that trains your baby, but more gently than the traditional Cry It Out method, and seems to me the easiest on both the parents and the baby.

Here's how to do it:

1. Get your baby into his own room

If you are starting sleep training at around six months, it's fine to allow your baby to fall asleep in his own room while the training is taking place. If your baby has been in your room up until this point, leave him there, but relocate temporarily to another part of the house or apartment yourself, even on a mattress in your living room, if you have nowhere else. Once your baby is sleeping better, you can move back into your bedroom.

If your baby has been sharing a room with an older child, move the older child into your room or another room for five nights or so (let them know that it won't be forever, just until the baby is sleeping better). Once the training is over, the child can move back in with the baby – and in fact, this often works very well for young children, who like having a sibling in the same room as them.

2. Remove all sleep aids

If you want your baby to learn to sleep, you will need to remove everything that they currently use to get back to sleep. This includes pacifiers, bottles of milk, rocking and patting and breastfeeding. Babies who have learned to sleep will still wake in the night from time to time, but won't require a bottle, breastfeed, pacifier or anything else to get back to sleep. If you want a good night's sleep, all of these aids have to go, or you'll continue being woken in the night for 'room service'.

3. Plan your approach

Sleep training should ideally take place once you have worked out a plan and talked it over with your partner, so you are both on the same page. Also, if you have close neighbours, let them know what's going on so they don't assume the baby is being left to cry. Pick a time that suits you, when the baby is well and you don't have other things going on.

4. Ensure you are well and happy, too

Don't try sleep training if you are under lots of pressure at work, or don't feel happy about it for some reason. Sleep training requires calm, confident parents, so get some extra rest in preparation, and make sure you are feeling calm and positive before you start. Think Calm, Confident, Consistent and you are on your way to better nights! If you are going to be falling apart, crying and feeling guilty, it's best not to even try sleep training, as it does take determination!

The First Night

Carry out your bedtime ritual as normal around 7.30pm, ensuring your baby has been up since at least 4pm, preferably earlier.

Put her to bed without any sleep aids. She will cry, but stay out of the room for a few minutes, then go back in and provide some brief reassurance, such as a stroke of the cheek or some gentle words, then leave again.

Remember, she now needs to get herself to sleep.

Go back in to your baby as often as you need to, but gradually lengthen the intervals until she falls asleep. Be prepared for some resistance – this may take an hour, or perhaps two, and there will be a lot of crying and yelling. Remind yourself of the benefits of everyone getting more unbroken sleep at night, if you feel yourself wavering.

She will also wake up during the night, particularly if she is used to having a breastfeed, bottle or pacifier. Rather than getting up and down all night, get out of bed when she wakes again, maybe have a cup of tea or watch some TV, and wait until she goes back to sleep again.

There may be quite a lot of crying on the first night. But by the third night of sleep training there will be less, and your baby should be sleeping well within five nights, after a small amount of 'wind-down' crying at bedtime.

How to Make Sure Your Baby Sleeps Through the Night

Once you have been through sleep training with your baby, you will naturally want to make sure it continues to work. The best way to ensure your baby does a lot of sleeping and very little waking at night (allowing for the odd disruption due to sickness or a developmental leap, for example), is to stay consistent. Here are some ways to make sure your baby sleeps through the night.

Don't reintroduce sleep aids

As part of your sleep training, you removed all external sleep aids, such as pacifiers, bottles of milk, and breastfeeding. Now that you have done that, don't reintroduce the pacifier or other aids, as it will only confuse your baby and set you back.

Babies who have learned to sleep on their own, without any external help, will continue to do so, and should make it through to morning without disturbing their parents at all. This may make daytime sleeps harder for a week or so, but they will soon improve too.

Don't change their nappy during the night

Once your baby is asleep, leave them be. There is no need to change nappies during the night.

Don't panic if they vomit

Sometimes, a baby may vomit during sleep training. This is no reason to give up, as babies do vomit very easily at times. If it happens, stay calm, clean your baby without too much fuss, and continue as you started. As long as you remain calm and consistent, your baby will quickly calm down.

Why Sleep Training Fails & What to Do

Sometimes sleep training simply doesn't work. This can be due to the baby's temperament or the fact that you simply can't bear to leave your baby to cry. Here are some common reasons for failure, and what you can do about them.

- Your living arrangements aren't suitable

If you have a very small apartment and share a room with your baby, it may be difficult to leave your baby to cry. Neighbours and other people living in your house who disagree with what you're doing can also make it hard. There are no easy answers here - you may need to wait a little longer, or work on sleep training your baby a little more slowly, with less crying. Options here include rocking, patting, a dummy and breastfeeding through the night, for example.

- Your baby puts up a strong fight

Some babies will react very strongly to sleep training and giving up their sleep aids. In some cases, this may mean that it takes longer. In others, you may feel that the crying and protests aren't worth it. It may take as long as seven days to see results, but as long as you are following the guidelines I have outlined above, and your baby doesn't seem to be getting more distressed, you can continue.

It may also be that your baby isn't ready. In this case, wait until he is a little older, perhaps nine or 10 months, and then try again.

- Lack of support from those around you

Sometimes sleep training fails because one parent isn't on board with the idea, or perhaps because other people, such as well-meaning friends and family, try and tell you it's a bad idea. If you can't come to a suitable compromise, or feel yourself wavering, again, it may be better to leave it for a few months and try again later. As always, listen to your own instincts here, as they will serve you better than well-meaning outsiders who don't understand your baby or your situation as well as you do. And have a chat to your health care provider if that helps.

- Lack of planning or it's just not the right time

As you can see from reading through the programme, you need to factor in a certain amount of broken sleep and disruption when sleep training. If you try and do it at a time when you have a lot of other things happening, or you haven't factored in how much energy it will take, it may not succeed. Again (are you seeing a theme here?), let it go if it's not working or you can't handle it right now, and try again later.

Personally, I don't think it's worth doing too much sleep training before six months of age. In my experience, you will get better results if you wait until your baby is eating well during the day, and more settled generally. Before then, managing on less sleep and adapting your lifestyle accordingly is a better option.

- Lack of consistency

If you let your baby into your bed one night, then the following night refuse to pick them up, and then give up after two hours, then it's fair to say that you aren't going to successfully sleep train your baby. Remember that babies don't find it easy to understand what you are trying to do, so being consistent is essential if you want a new habit to stick. They will go along with what you want eventually, but they need to know what that is.

- You haven't got the day sleeps under control

If you don't have consistent day sleeps, you will struggle to implement any kind of routine at night. As I have stated earlier, always work on your daytime routine and your bedtime ritual before you try and tackle nights. If this is fairly consistent, sleep training should be much easier.

- Your check ups are too stimulating

When you go into to check on your baby, take care not to be too over-the-top in your attention. Remain calm and reassuring, but keep your visit as brief and simple as possible so that you don't overstimulate or further distress your baby. You want him to feel safe and reassured by your presence, but also able to put himself to sleep – a tricky balance, and one that may be easier with your second baby, if you have one.

Chapter 6 - It's Naptime!

Good day sleeps are another important need for babies through their first year. The patterns of napping will change and eventually your baby will have their own established routine. Getting this right, and prioritising naps so that they don't miss this important rest time, is key to good sleeping at night.

One question new parents often ask is if naptime can interfere with bedtime. Generally, no. While a very late nap – for example, waking up after 4pm, can lead to a later bedtime – for most babies, good naps during the day mean they aren't overtired at night and will find it easier to drift off to sleep.

If you get your baby down for his afternoon nap at time that allows for two 45-minute sleep cycles and a wake-up time of around 3pm, you should be fine for bedtime. And, of course, some lucky parents have a baby who can sleep until 5pm and still be back in bed by 7pm.

Babies change so quickly throughout their first year, and that 'good sleeper' you bring home from the hospital will soon be awake much more, and need more help to get back to sleep for daytime naps. Read on for a guide to how many naps your baby should be having throughout their first year and beyond.

Newborns (up to six weeks of age) should be having three to five naps a day, with 30 to 90 minutes awake time between each nap. There will be one nap in the morning and one or two in the afternoon, with perhaps a couple of short 'catnaps' thrown in, too.

Babies from six to 15 weeks of age should be having three to four naps a day, with one or two hours of awake time between each nap.

Babies aged four to six months need three naps a day, with lengthening awake times of 1.5 to 2.5 hours between each nap.

Babies aged six to eight months need two to three naps a day, with two to three hours of awake time between each nap.

Babies aged eight to ten months need one to two naps a day, with two to three hours between each nap. Generally, babies who wake very early (between five am and six am) will keep having two sleeps for longer. If they sleep a little later in the morning, they will transition to one sleep a day more quickly.

Babies aged 10-12 months plus need one to two naps a day, with 2.5 to 3.5 hours of awake time between each nap.

After the first birthday, your baby may continue to have two sleeps, but many will have a single, longer nap after lunch, and this can continue until they are aged three or even four. But some toddlers will drop their day sleeps quite early, which can be disappointing for parents who rely on that time to get a few things done and enjoy some peace and quiet. Read on for a few strategies to deal with babies and toddlers who refuse to nap.

Strategies for a Successful Naptime

When your baby is very small, naps will happen without you needing to do much more beyond feeding, cuddling and soothing them to sleep, perhaps in your arms or close by in bed.

You may wish to try and get them into a routine, but many parents find that their naps and awake times change so quickly that by the time they are used to one routine, their baby no longer plays along – such as when the morning nap is dropped.

Once they are around six months though, when they are settled, eating three meals and day and moving more, it can be a good idea to time daytime naps more precisely so that your baby is up and busy again well before bedtime. And, as I've mentioned earlier, sorting out your day time routine is essential for successful sleep training at night at this age.

Here are some key ways to ensure that naps are successful:

Pay attention to your baby's natural sleep cycle, and time naps accordingly.

Look for signs of tiredness – rubbing eyes, signs of unhappiness, clenched fists, avoiding eye contact – and move your baby towards their sleeping area before they get really upset, feeding first to fill them up before sleep.

Have a designated sleeping area and take them there once they are ready to nap. We have covered this already, but it should be warm but not overheated, dark, quiet and peaceful. Putting your baby to sleep in the same place for every nap may work well for babies who 'fight sleep' as it sets up strong sleep associations and signals to them that it's time for bed.

For daytime naps, a blackout blind may be helpful in encouraging your baby to drop off, and some parents swear by a strict nap schedule (for example, at 12 noon every day for exactly) to ensure that the day nap happens and bedtime isn't disrupted. As with many things, only you will be able to work out what will suit you lifestyle and your baby's temperament and sleep patterns.

Others may fall asleep in the car and readily transfer to a pram or their own bed. With my first son I used to let him fall asleep in the car, then move him gently to his pram and let him have his sleep there, so I could go to the library or a cafe and have some time to myself. This worked for me, but it won't work for all babies and toddlers, who may struggle to 'transfer' to a pram or their own bed during a nap.

Choose what works for you and your baby – the time when they are asleep is a well-deserved break for you, too, so ideally you want them to get a good, long sleep at this time so you get a break, too.

Leave them alone to fall asleep - as with sleep training at night, you sometimes need to leave your baby alone for a few minutes to actually drop off to sleep. Some babies need time to unwind and fuss a little before dropping off, so leave your baby to it and see what happens. If your baby becomes distressed, you can try picking him up, soothing etc, and then try again to put him down, drowsy and relaxed, but still awake, to see if he will fall asleep on his own.

Be consistent. Working your day around your baby's naps takes some planning, but can make life much easier. Get out and about when they are awake and happy, then be home for naptime so that they get a good long sleep and you get some time to yourself. Knowing when they need to be down for their nap so that they get a good sleep but are still up in time for their evening routine and set bedtime means that night sleeping will fall into place more easily, too.

Don't let them nap for too long, or too late. Some babies are still confused about night and day, and will sleep for too long during the day, then be alert at night. Try to limit late afternoon naps from around six months of age, getting them down for sleep earlier so you know they will have time to get through the early evening and bedtime routine without dropping off again.

While I don't believe in waking a sleeping baby (why would you?) I think it's worth timing naps so that you have some consistency when your baby will be ready for bed at night. This also ensures that your baby is getting enough sleep, which is so critical for development.

What if Your Baby Won't Nap?

Some babies and toddlers will go through tricky phases when they won't nap during the day, no matter how exhausted and grumpy they may seem. Sometimes, this can mean you need to look at bedtime and move it a little earlier or a little later and see if this helps. And some days are just more challenging than others.

If your baby hasn't had enough stimulation or exercise they may resist naptime. Here, some activity can help, such as going for a swim in a heated pool, or to a playground or playgroup. Lots of chatter, singing and engagement with them will also ready them for a good sleep. Being consistent, remaining calm and keeping an eye out for sleep cues may also help. As soon as your baby seems relaxed and drowsy, take him in to his sleeping area and see if he will drop off.

Also, some babies and toddlers will stop napping at around one year to 15 months, apart from perhaps the odd catnap. This does make the day long for parents, but if it's what your baby chooses, there's not much you can do about it. Encouraging 'quiet time' after lunch can mean you still get a break – leaving them in their room with an audio book playing, or with a few books and toys, for example. And ideally bed time will be earlier if your baby or toddler has been awake all day.

Signs that your baby or toddler is ready to drop their daytime nap are generally that the child simply refuses to sleep, even if you put him in his cot. He may play, scream or cry out. And after a week or so the parent realises the nap is not going to happen. There may be a week or two of unsettled, overtired behaviour, but eventually you and your child will both adjust to the new routine.

You may also decide to stop the daytime sleep yourself if your baby is up until 9pm at night and you are no longer getting any time to yourself in the evenings. You may choose to live with this, or you may decide to drop the daytime nap in exchange for an early bedtime – it's up to you.

If you do have a baby who doesn't sleep during the day, I recommend pursuing a sleep training programme at night. You may not be able to force your baby to sleep during the day, but that is all the more reason to assume that they can and will sleep well at night. Often, sorting out night time sleeping can help with day sleeps, too. And even if they don't, and your baby or toddler has definitely given up their day nap, or only has brief catnaps, at least everyone is getting a good sleep at night.

Remember also that so many of these problems will vanish in a few years' time and you won't even remember them. Your children will be at school, come home exhausted, and fall into bed without too much drama. So don't despair too much if you have a 'bad sleeper' – it's not your fault, and it will pass!

Chapter 7 - No Problem Too Big

In this chapter we'll cover the dreaded sleep regressions that occur as your baby moves through babyhood and toddler months. They aren't as scary as they sound, they, and will pass quickly. But until they do, there are a few things you can try that will make life easier in the meantime.

We'll also look at how to work on establishing good sleep habits when you are parenting alone. And finally, we'll cover sleep when you have twins. In both of these scenarios, parents need extra support, and there are ways of making it easier for yourself.

Understanding Sleep Regressions by Age

Sleep regression is something you will come up against a few times as your baby moves towards toddlerhood. It's totally normal, and is characterised by your baby waking up frequently when previously she had been sleeping well. Daytime naps might be difficult; you might feel like you've barely had any sleep because she was up and down all night, fretting and crying. Your baby might also seem grumpy, fretful and more clingy than usual.

Sleep regressions tend to last from about two weeks to six weeks if you're unlucky. Although sleep regression can be difficult, especially if everything has been going well up until that point, they are part of your baby's rapid development at this time, and means that they are healthy, thriving and growing as they should be.

Sleep regressions mostly occur at four, nine, 18 and 36 months of age – which are also times when your baby is changing rapidly and going through a lot of physical and cognitive development. One thing you will notice is that babies and toddlers don't change gradually – they seem the same for a while, and then all of a sudden they may be eating more, seem unsettled, or sleeping deeply, and then you'll find they have changed quite rapidly, thanks to a big growth spurt. One of the biggest transformations is around the age of three, when your toddler transforms into a very small child – and this stage is also characterised by a final sleep regression.

While not all babies and toddlers experience dramatic sleep regressions, most parents do notice a change in sleeping patterns around these ages, and it helps to be prepared for it. Read on for more information about sleep regressions by age.

The Four Month Sleep Regression

This sleep regression is when babies change from their newborn pattern of active sleep followed by deep sleep, into a new pattern of cycling through REM, light and active sleep. You may notice some unsettled behaviour and clinginess, some poor sleep at night, and also greater focus from your baby – he or she suddenly seems more alert, and more like a person. This is a lovely age and a small sleep regression won't matter so much when you noticed so much more joy and engagement from your baby!

The Nine Month Sleep Regression

The regression at nine months occurs at around the same time your baby develops "object permanence," which is the understanding that someone or something still exists even if your baby can't see them. This can also cause some separation anxiety, which is why your previously happy baby will now weep when you go to the shower, for example. Even if you have successfully sleep trained your baby at around six months, she will now wake up and realise that you're not there and start to cry, wanting you to be near her.

Let her know that you are leaving the room and will come back, rather than suddenly disappearing. This will make it easier for her and help her understand that when you go, you always come back. This may make nighttime separation anxiety less troubling, too.

Around this time babies also have a significant growth spurt as they move towards toddlerhood. They will start standing, crawling and moving around. You may notice your baby practising these skills in a half-sleep state, which obviously interferes with bedtime. Be assured, it will pass! And once they are on the move, they will sleep better at night, too.

The 18 Month Sleep Regression

This is another period of rapid change for your toddler – he or she is becoming more independent and starting to think about how he relates to others more. With a new social and emotional awareness comes increased anxiety and perhaps some disrupted sleep.

The 36 Month Sleep Regression

Much like the regression at 18 months, this period in your toddler's life is characterised by a huge leap in development and growth, both emotional and physical. Your little one may be starting pre-school, and is also likely to be talking lots, moving lots and spending time with other children more. New emotions, such as jealousy, can also take time to work through, particularly as this is often a time when a new sibling appears on the scene.

Toddlers are also learning a huge amount right now – which can make it hard for them to settle down to sleep. The world around them becomes fascinating – everything from leaves to worms to water is a source of constant information, and you'll be hearing the word 'why?' a lot, too. Dreams and imagination are taking off, along with fears both rational and irrational.

All of these factors can increase anxiety and lead to some unsettled nights until your child settles into his new 'self.'

How to Deal With Sleep Regressions

If your baby is very young, you will need to provide extra reassurance and cuddles until the sleep regression passes. Look after your own needs, too, until your baby is more settled, and get more sleep and rest as needed, much as you did when your baby was a newborn.

If you have already sleep trained at around six months, try not to abandon everything your baby has learned. Ideally, you will provide extra care and soothing as necessary, without moving them into your bed, or giving up on letting your baby drift off to sleep alone permanently. While it may not feel like it at the time, sleep regressions do pass. Staying in the room a little longer may be all you need to do to help your baby through this stage.

If you do end up co-sleeping or cuddling your baby to sleep for a while, you may need to do some sleep training again once the regression is over – see how you go. Some tummy or head stroking, with some soothing sounds and your presence, may be all that's required, keeping to your routine of putting your baby down drowsy, but awake.

As always, keep the sleeping area dark and quiet, to give your baby the clear message that it's time to sleep. Now is a good time to demonstrate, again, that nights are a little boring, too – turn off all screens, and ensure that there's nothing too interesting happening in your house at bedtime.

Sometimes, checking in on your baby during the night and offering a stroke and a kiss may reassure them that you are there, preventing more upset later.

For sleep regressions in older babies and toddlers, also ensure that they are getting plenty of time during the day to practise new skills, such as gross motor skills. Set up an "obstacle course" in your home for them to crawl and climb over, or take them to a baby-friendly play centre and let them do some exploring. Giving them lots of opportunity to work on new skills and wear themselves out in the day time can make a big difference to your nights.

You'll also need to offer more emotional support during the day. She's feeling more adventurous and independent, but this can lead to some anxiety too. Extra attention, lots of cuddles and cosy time with books and a blanket will all make a big difference. Give her opportunities to discharge all that emotion with laughter, play and even some tears while you hold and soothe her – she'll be much happier after a good cry.

The main thing to remember is that your baby will need some extra support at this time, and the more you are able to offer, the easier and more smoothly the sleep regression will go.

If In Doubt, Seek Help

As always, if your instincts are troubling you, see your paediatrician if you feel like the sleep regression is going on for too long, or your child seems really distressed. Talking to your doctor will rule out any larger problems, and help to set your mind at ease.

Look After Yourself

If you are feeling exhausted by your child's sleep regression, be sure to cancel any unnecessary commitments and get some extra sleep yourself. As always, you need to fill your own cup up as a parent before you can take care of your child's needs properly. So eat well, have some early nights and soon it will pass.

6 Must-Know Sleep Strategies for Single Parents

If you are parenting a baby alone, first of all know that my heart goes out to you! Read on for some sleep strategies to help single parents get through those early weeks with a newborn, and through the times that follow.

Call On Help

If you can, call on family or friends to help you get through the early months with your baby. Just having someone take the baby from you for a few hours so you can get some extra sleep in the mornings will make a huge difference to your energy levels. If you can afford it, a night nurse will also be invaluable in helping you through the newborn stage. Or even someone who can come in during the day and hold the baby for a few hours, or walk it around the block, while you have a rest or just stare into space.

Gather a Support Network

If you're a single parent, you'll have times when you are managing fine, and times when you need a bit of extra help, for example when you get sick. Work on building up a reliable local support network within your community so that you can call on someone when you are having a bad week, and return the favour when they need help from you. Join online community groups, go to mother's groups, and ask your local child health centre about what kind of support is available to single parents in your area. If you have space, an au pair or student who can help out a little in exchange for accommodation is another option that may work for you.

Sleep When Your Baby Sleeps

Easier said than done, I know, particularly when you have lots of other things to do in your spare time. But worth doing for your health and your energy levels. If you don't want to sleep through every nap time, just do it when you can. Or once or twice a week, go to bed at night when your baby does, so you can catch up on sleep that way.

If you find it hard to sleep during the day, at least try and enjoy your free time when you can. Rather than doing housework, call a friend, or have a relaxing bath, or read a book with a cup of tea – whatever you need to unwind.

Consider Whether Co-sleeping Might Work For You

As we have discussed in earlier chapters, co-sleeping can often work with clingy babies who don't like to be separated from their parents. If you think this is a good idea, try setting up a cot next to your bed with an open side so your baby has a safe place to sleep, yet is still close to you. This will make nighttime feeds and wakings much easier when you don't get a respite or have someone else to share the night feeds.

Get To Know Other Single Parents

You'll soon find other people in the same position as you, who can sympathise with the challenges of lone parenting. Find groups online or in real life where you can have a laugh and talk and share tips without judgement. You're not alone – you just need to find your community! The great thing about online communities for parents is that they are global, so there's always someone to talk to, even in the middle of the night.

Be Aware of Your Mental Health

Single parenting is a tough gig at times, so it's important to be vigilant about your own health and wellbeing. Know the signs of postpartum depression, and keep in regular contact with your family doctor. Always seek help if you find yourself struggling. Keep a list of phone numbers for parenting helplines and health services close to and so you can always get support, should you need it.

Working On Your Baby's Sleep as a Single Parent

Much of what we have already covered remains the same when you are parenting alone. But here are some tips to help you with your baby's sleep that are both realistic and will make life much easier for you.

- A simple, manageable bedtime routine will help you feel in control. While this is helpful for all parents, I think it's particularly important for single parents who will find the routine stops them from being overwhelmed – and of course it's great for lone parents to get some time to themselves in the evenings, so don't feel bad about putting your baby to be early and sleep training at six months, should you need to!

- Have a sleepover with a relative or friend who can give you a break from early morning wake-ups. Ideally, it should be someone who will help out with some light housework, get up early or in the night, and provide some emotional support. One day, you will return the favour, so take all help that's offered! It's important to ask, as sometimes people don't really know what you need. And again, seek out any support services on offer within your community, too.

Two Babies, Many Solutions

If you have twins, you may be wondering if you can try sleep training at all. After all, if it's difficult to get one baby to sleep, how on earth will you manage with two? As with lone parenting, you may find that establishing and following a set routine makes it easier for you to manage this added responsibility. And again, don't be afraid to ask for help, including from local services set up to support families with twins and more. Also, take heart. While teaching two babies to sleep might seem much harder, you can and will get there. Here are some tips, often sourced from parents who have raised twins themselves.

Set the Same Bedtime for Both

What you want to do here is synchronise your babies' sleep cycles so that they are awake and asleep at around the same times. Otherwise, one or the other will always be awake, and you will soon be exhausted. Fortunately, twins are naturally in tune with one another, so here you can work with their natural inclination to be close. The principles here are much the same as sleep training single babies.

Always Settle The Calmer Baby First

You probably know this already, but if not, always work on your calmer baby first, to allow you uninterrupted time with the fussy one a little later. This will mean your calm baby gets your attention and hopefully drifts off to sleep, and therefore doesn't miss out on the attention her or she needs.

If one starts fussing, check on the quiet one first to make sure she's happy, then deal with the fussy one. This will help both babies to feel loved and happy. And don't panic if one starts screaming – often, twins aren't bothered by the other one's cry, even if they are in the same room.

Put your twins to be when they are awake, but drowsy

Here again, you can start some simple sleep training even when your twins are quite small by putting them into their safe sleeping space when they are still awake. They will hopefully drift off to sleep, leaving you with some much-needed alone time. You won't be able to rock two babies to sleep for long, so putting your babies down to sleep is going to be a decision that is made for you, to a certain degree. You can still give them cuddles while they are awake, perhaps a couple of board books and a lullaby, and soon they will learn to drift off on their own, in their own bed. Ideally your partner should be around to help with bedtimes in the early months.

Try Swaddling Your Babies

Swaddling can work well for all babies, but is particularly helpful when it works for twins (I say when, because not all babies like being swaddled.) It makes babies feel safe, 'held,' and ready for sleep, and they are after all used to being very tightly packed into a small space! You will need to stop at around two months of age, but at this point you can swap to zip-up baby sleeping bags for the same sleep association and secure feeling.

Keep Nights Boring and Quiet

As with all babies, you want to discourage them from seeing night as anything other than a time to sleep. During the day, cuddle and talk to them as much as you like. But keep night-time interactions, light, cuddles and chatter to a minimum, so they are clear on the fact that nights are not play time. This is important with all babies, but particularly important with twins, when you have two babies to settle, not just one. Twins may also like a cuddly toy or some comfort object to hold onto at night from around one year of age.

Black-out blinds, lullaby CDs and white noise machines are another thing that may twin parents find very handy when getting two babies to sleep. Draw on everything you can find, and you'll find it much easier!

Accept That Your Twins May Have Different Sleep Needs

If you find that your twins sleep differently, which is common, you may need to treat them differently. Some parents put their twins in separate rooms, as one is a better sleeper than the other. As with all aspects of parenting, as long is it's safe, it's up to you. One waking up is always better than two waking up, so whatever works!

You may need to separate them into separate rooms to sleep train at around six months, and then put them back in the same room once you've managed this and they are sleeping well again. Or you might get them to sleep each night in separate rooms and then move them into one room later on in the night – up to you. The sooner you get them sleeping in a way that will work for you all long term, the better for your family as a whole. As always, go easy on yourself and ask for help when you need it.

With daytime naps, it may be that you need to soothe one to sleep first, and then the other, so one wakes around around 20 minutes earlier than the second. This is part of life with twin babies – to some extent you need to be flexible and let go of expectations. You just need to do everything one baby at a time and be patient. It will get easier!

Set Up A Sleep Schedule

More so than with one baby, with twins it's absolutely critical that parents are getting enough sleep. It shouldn't be one person getting up to do all the night wakings, it should be both. Setting up a timetable or schedule will help to ensure that no one becomes too sleep deprived. Obviously you'll need to take into account the needs of your own family, and work commitments.

Call in Help

If you can afford it, get some help, particularly in the early days. A night nurse, a cleaner, even someone to cook a few healthy meals – whatever it takes to get you through. A live-in au pair is another option that can work well.

Online parenting forums specifically for twins are another invaluable source of tips and support, as are multiple birth associations, so get on board with all of these as soon as you know you are expecting twins.

Streamline Everything

Have as much done in advance as you can – for example, bottles sterilised, nappies stocked up, sleeping bags laid out before you bring each baby out of the bath at night. Meal plan, have a weekly online shop, get regular help… whatever it takes to simplify your life! And be sure to schedule in some time for yourself, too – when you are parenting twins, this isn't a luxury, it's essential.

Chapter 8 - Completing Your No-Cry Toolkit

In our final chapter, we'll look at some common problems that come up with babies, and how you can work through them. These include how to soothe a crying baby – giving you lots of hints and strategies. We'll also look at colic – what it is, what helps, and how you can help your baby work through it. And finally, we'll look at how you can help your baby sleep better when he or she is not feeling well.

How to Soothe a Crying Baby

Learning to soothe a crying baby is something you learn on the job, and when you have a baby who cries a lot, it can be very tough on a new parent. You may wonder what's wrong with your baby, or that you are going to lose control and harm your baby or that you aren't connecting with your baby. I remember fearing, as a very new mother, that my baby was scared of me and that was why he was crying! It can feel like a rejection, but it really isn't. It's simply your baby getting used to being in the world. Once you establish some basic feeding and sleeping routines, and your baby is a little bigger, it will all get much easier.

In the meantime, learning a few techniques to soothe a crying baby will help you get through the bad days. Firstly, let's look at why babies cry so much, as this knowledge can help parents feel better able to manage it and not feel overwhelmed.

So why do babies cry so much?

All babies cry. But in truth, no one can say for sure exactly why babies. It may be to do with hunger, or bellyaches, or overtiredness. They can't talk, so they can't tell us exactly what the problem is, unfortunately. Crying is their way of gaining our attention and focus, which they need to survive when they are so small and helpless. But over time, you will learn to recognise some of your baby's unique crying patterns and what they mean – and then you will be able to meet their needs so the crying soon stops.

And in fact, it's important to remember that a healthy baby should and will cry regularly. If your baby never cries, you should seek advice from your family doctor.

Some common reasons for crying include:

- Tiredness and overstimulation; need for sleep
- Needing a new diaper
- Feeling hungry
- Colic, reflux or food intolerances
- Pain or sickness
- Gas
- Fear or a sudden loud noise may lead to crying
- No apparent reason

As a parent, it can be hard to deal with a crying baby for hours on end, particularly when you are tired and emotional yourself. But a certain amount of crying is completely normal for all babies, and some cry a lot more than others.

What you need to bear in mind, too, is that excessive crying can be very hard on you as a parent, especially if you are someone who tends to be quite hard on yourself. You may feel that you 'should' be able to deal with your baby and you are doing something wrong if you can't stop him crying. But in fact, by simply being there, holding your baby and letting him know you are there, you are doing everything right.

The early days and weeks where there may be a lot of crying will soon pass and in the meantime, you just need to go easy on yourself and get as much rest as you can. Unexplained crying builds from birth, tends to peak at about six weeks of age, and tapers off by three months. Mark your calendar and look forward to that magic date when the crying stops – it will come.

Having said that, if your baby seems like they are in pain, or you sense that something is wrong, always seek medical help. Trust your instincts.

Baby Crying Patterns by Age

Birth to three weeks: At this age, many babies sleep a lot and cry for only short periods of time, usually due to hunger or tiredness.

Three weeks to 12 weeks: At this point, babies tend to cry more and sleep less. There may be some periods of crying due to hunger or overtiredness, which are easily solved with sleep, a feed or some gentle soothing. And there may be some periods of unexplained crying where nothing seems to help. For some babies, there is a lot of crying, for no apparent reason, that goes on for a few months, often until three or six months of age. This occurs with around 20 per cent of babies, unfortunately. By six months, most babies are much happier and more settled in the world.

Often the diagnosis is 'colic', which is a kind of catch-all term for the unsettled crying and apparent stomach pain that many babies seem to show when they crying a lot, writhe and howl after feeding. Often, there may be more crying in the evening, that can go on for a couple of hours before sleep descends. And sometimes there may be a bad day when it feels like your baby does nothing but cry.

Here are some effective remedies for colic that you may find useful. There are no proven treatments for colic, because the causes can be so hard to pinpoint in individual babies, mostly because they are so young and change so quickly. But you can try and lesson their discomfort and distress so that the episode passes more quickly, and in trying different things you may be able to pinpoint what is causing them it to some extent.

5 Effective Remedies for Colic

Lay your baby on his tummy

You can do this across your lap, on the floor on a rug, or more upright along your chest. You can also gently rub his back, which might help with any digestive discomfort. Tummy time will also help to strengthen neck and shoulder muscles, but you should only do this when your baby is awake and you are there to keep an eye on him or he

Work on good sleep

Of course I would say this! But it's true – sorting out good sleep is the key to sorting out a lot of your baby's unsettled behaviour. And very small babies have an added difficulty in that they find it hard to 'hold still' enough to go to sleep, often jerking themselves awake as they drop off. Swaddling, rocking and even "wearing" your baby in a sling are all ways to hold them still enough to soothe their distress and let them fall asleep. Another trick is to walk the floor with your baby – wrap them up or put them in a sling, and the pace up and down until they drop off. If you know they are well fed and there aren't any underlying health issues, it's fine to wear headphones may block out the crying until they fall asleep.

Another problem is of course that babies can only stay away for a short period of time before they get grumpy and restless, and they then need to calm down enough to fall asleep – but are crying too much to manage this! This is something that they will learn to do over time, and meanwhile they need your patience and support.

Introduce a pacifier

You may find that your baby is much happier and able to calm themselves down with a pacifier. Yes, you will need to get rid of it at some point, but many parents find it gives them some much needed relief from crying.

Give a warm bath before bed

A long, warm bath will often calm a crying baby – the water, the sounds and the soothing hands holding them will all help to settle colic and fretful behaviour. A massage in dark, warm room with a scented oil, some cuddling, and gentle white noise may also help to soothe a colicky baby.

Gentle handling

When your baby is very unhappy and colicky, be sure to handle them with firm, steady movements, without any jerking or hard back-patting. Sharp movements will alarm your baby and cause more screaming and upset. Another reason small babies become upset is if they are handed between lots of different people. Sometimes, if your baby becomes overstimulated retreating to a dark, quiet room can help.

What they need more than anything is a calm, safe environment with you. They have just arrived in the world, after all, and it can be frightening.

Oddly enough, some parents report that holding their baby a lot during the day gives rise to easier evenings. Babies love being held, rocked, and close to you, so if you leave them in their pram all day they may "hand you a bill" later and demand a few hours of your undivided attention in the evening. If you find you have a very clingy, colicky baby, a sling can help you get a few things done without having to put your baby down.

An important point: This need for attention never really goes away – your children will always want your attention, and pre-empting this need with lots of loving attention will prevent them trying to gain it with acting out, or giving up and "looking for love in all the wrong places" later on.

Manage your own wellbeing with a colicky baby

When it comes to colicky babies, it's also helpful to manage this phase (which won't last long, but may feel like it's going to last for ever) by taking good care of yourself. Ask for support and help from those you trust, who won't make comments about your howling baby, and take any food, babysitting offers or help with cleaning that comes your way.

- Do you have someone who can come over and just hold the baby for a while so you can have a shower and some time to yourself?

- Can you get a cleaner or some other help with housework so you don't have to live in a mess, which can be very stressful?

- Can you put in some headphones and let the baby cry for a while in his bed while you take a bit of time out? A healthy baby can be left to cry for short periods of time quite safely, and may even drop off to sleep if left alone.

- Look after yourself. A crying baby can be exhausting, so as always, prioritise your own wellbeing and you will feel better able to cope with your baby. Eat well, get enough rest, and avoid alcohol and smoking and you will feel better able to cope with this stage in your life.

Is it a medical problem?

No one really knows. Some babies may suffer from reflux or other stomach upsets or be particularly sensitive to a particular formula milk, or something their mother has eaten if they are breastfed. Some mothers may try eliminating certain foods, such as chillies, spicy food, coffee, garlic or dairy – there's no harm in trying and seeing what happens.

Helping a Sick Baby Get Restful Sleep

Another aspect of living with a baby that you will have to get used to is occasional sickness, at least until their immune system has built up a little. The first year of daycare can also be rough, as your baby will bring home lots of bugs and germs he hasn't been exposed to before. Lack of hygiene and a tendency to explore and put fingers in mouths also leads to lots of not-so-lovely germs being shared around. You might noticed earaches (lots of screaming and head-banging), colds, blocked noses, feverishness and upset stomachs.

Of course, most serious illnesses can be prevented by immunisation, but colds and sniffles will still appear, and can also lead to some broken nights, sadly. Often, a sick baby will be in pain and will find it impossible to sleep. Yet sleep is exactly what they need to fight off illness and recover. What you need to do is decrease their discomfort to the point that they can sleep soundly without aches and pains keeping them (and you) up.

Here are some ways you can help your baby or toddler get a good night's sleep when they are ill:

- Use a humidifier. This will ease breathing difficulties and reduce the chance of your baby waking up due to congestion.
- Use an over-the-counter painkiller for children. Talk to your pharmacist about the best one to use and follow the instructions for correct dosages very carefully. Some babies and toddlers will happily swallow a liquid treatment, others may need a suppository. Never give more than the recommended dose – keep note of how much you have given and when.
- Allow for extra naps in the daytime to make up for broken sleep at night. Extra rocking, cuddling and attention is also going to help your baby feel better, as sickness can make them miserable and clingy. On the same note, start the bedtime routine a little earlier and make sure your baby doesn't get cold when you bathe him or her – keep a towel in the bathroom and dress him there straight away to prevent chills, and make the

water nice and steamy to help clear his nose. Sometimes, sitting in a steamy bathroom can help, too.
- A vapor rub on his chest can ease breathing and feels nice, too. You can make your own by mixing up four teaspoons of grated beeswax with three tablespoons of cocoa or shea butter, seven tablespoons of coconut oil and 30 drops off essential oil – ten drops eucalyptus oil, ten drops tea tree oil, five drops lavender oil and five drops chamomile oil is a lovely blend that will clear a blocked nose and promote sleep.
- Saline nose drops, available from the pharmacist, can help to clear a blocked nose, though your baby may protest loudly.
- Propping up your baby's mattress slightly, by putting a pillow under the mattress, will also help to ease a blocked nose and the pain of an ear infection. Only do this with babies that are six months old and upwards.
- Keep your baby hydrated, either with extra breastfeeds or bottles, as needed. Older babies might prefer watered-down juice or milk – whatever keeps them drinking fluid.
- If your baby vomits in bed, clean her up as quickly and calmly as you can, keeping lights low if possible. You may also like to clean out her mouth a little to get rid of the bad taste.
- Extra skin-to-skin contact is very good for sick babies, and is proven to speed up recovery. Hold your baby against your skin and remember that she will soon feel better.

Once the sickness passed

You may need to work a little to get back into your old sleep routine, but don't let all your progress be undone by a single bout of illness. Once your baby is feeling better, go back to leaving him to fall asleep in his cot, even if you've been rocking him to sleep during his illness. Babies are fast learners and you should be able to get back on track quickly as long as you remain calm and consistent.

Preventing another illness

While illness is simply part of childhood, and something you have to accept to some degree, you also want to prevent your child catching a serious illness that will affect his development. Here are some tips to prevent illness from rearing its head too often:

- First and most importantly, immunise your child according to his schedule. This is the best, and sometimes the only way to prevent serious childhood illnesses such as measles, mumps and rubella.
- Be sure to live in a smoke-free home and avoid smoke-filled areas to keep your children's lungs clear.
- Always wash your hands when you get home from anywhere. Over time, your child will watch you and will become a good hand washer on their own. Provide a stool in the bathroom so your child can access water and soap easily.
- Wash towels, sheets and all bedding frequently.
- Avoid sharing cups, cutlery and so on.
- Breastfeeding for the first 12 months is a great way to pass on your own immunity to germs that you encounter.
- Eat lots of fresh fruit and vegetables to boost immunity. Once your baby is moving onto solids, ensure their diet is full of vitamins, too.
- If your child is sick, don't go to playdates, playgrounds or public places such as libraries. Stay at home until it passes and don't spread the germs.

- Remember that childhood illness is normal and part of your baby building up his immune system – it will pass.

A final point: Sometimes, sleep problems can feel insurmountable. Let's say you've read this entire book, tried everything I have recommended, and your baby is still not sleeping well. As I have said throughout, this will change with time. But if you find you are feeling continually worried and stressed about your baby's lack of sleep, and the impact it is having on your, don't be afraid to seek help from a child health expert, such as your family doctor.

Occasionally, sleep problems can point to wider problems within the family, or even post-natal depression, and you will need to deal with these issues before you tackle sleep. If this rings true for you, and you've found it impossible to put into place a sleep training method, then perhaps you need to seek further help. It is there if you need it.

But generally, like everything to do with babies and toddlers, as long as the basics are there – lots of love, patience, support for parents and an understanding of baby and toddler behaviour – sleep should fall into place, if not straight away, then eventually. In the meantime, look after yourself at all times, because as a parent, your little one depends on your completely, and your health and wellbeing is the foundation of stable, thriving family life.

Conclusion

I hope this book has given you a lot to work with, and you now feel ready to handle your baby's sleep problems and to attempt sleep training if you feel it's the best option for your family. As you can see, there are no perfect solutions when it comes to baby and toddler sleep, and I have tried at all times to emphasise that this is a stage that will pass, and as a parent you are well-equipped to find your own ways to manage. Some toddlers and babies are just better sleepers than others – it's often a matter of luck, but you can improve things with some work and planning.

We looked first as sleep patterns by age, and what is normal for each stage. This is great for helping you see that what may feel like problems are actually totally normal and will pass with time. We also looked at how to set up a safe sleeping space for your baby, which is more important than anything else. Here we also covered sleep aids, such as monitors, night lights, blackout blinds and white noise machines, and when these might be a good idea.

Next we covered sleep associations – what they are and how to create them. And we looked at a basic routine that you can put in place to help with good sleeping, both during the day and at night. As always, a busy day and a structured, loving and fun routine is ideal for creating the right conditions for peaceful night sleeping.

In chapter three, we looked at sleep problems by age, both common and less common, and then we moved onto sleep training in chapter four, and how to choose the right method for your baby. We also covered tips for success, and how you might decide that the time is right for sleep training, such as if you are returning to work or you are simply feeling exhausted and want to tackle sleep problems a little.

We also looked at why six months is the perfect time to first try sleep training. You now know that the longer a baby or toddler is used to behaving in a certain way, such as being rocked to sleep, the more they will struggle to give it up. By the time a toddler is two, getting him to stop falling asleep in your bed, or on the couch, is going to be a lot harder. Changing the routine later on is going to involve a lot more resistance, and a lot more pain. Having said that, if you remain calm and consistent, sleep training will usually succeed at any age. It's just that six months is the first and often the best time to try it. After that, as your baby turns into a toddler, it may not be quite so easy, and your child will also be able to climb out of their cot and use their words to make you feel like a terrible parent, so it may be better to start sooner!

Next, we dived into the main techniques for sleep training – Fading Out, Crying it Out, Pick Up Put Down and Camping Out. We looked at which babies (and parents) are best suited to each method, and why Fading Out is the one that is most likely to succeed for many families. We then looked at why, unfortunately, sleep training might fail, and what to do if that happens. Often, it's simply a case of trying again later. And, remember, as always, that if it doesn't work, or you find it too hard, then you may go back to whatever you've been doing and forget about it entirely, knowing that you tried. As the parent, it's your call.

In Chapter Six we covered nap times for different ages, and why good daytime naps are key to sound sleeping at night. We also looked at what to do if your baby won't nap. Next we moved on to sleep regression, and how to handle them at each stage, and importantly, why they happen. As with so much of parenting, knowing what is developmentally normal can make it a lot easier to deal with. Here, we also looked at how single parents, and those look after twins, can manage sleep, naps and parenting in general – the two key tips here, and for all parents, are to look after yourself and seek help if you need to.

Lastly, we looked at crying babies – what crying means, how to soothe it, how to deal with colic in the early weeks. We then covered how to manage sickness and sleep, and how to prevent childhood illness as much as possible.

I hope that you now have a lot of information and confidence to deal with your baby's sleep. While there is no magic secret to great sleep in the early months, there is a lot you can do to move things in the right direction. Try not to beat yourself up, though, if you find it difficult coping on broken sleep while also trying to get on with other elements of your life, such as work and other relationships. It's normal, in the early years, to be functioning on very little sleep and not feeling full of energy, and many other parents are in the same boat. If anything, these years will teach you to be a little bit more understanding of those around you who seem tired and out of sorts – they may well have a very small baby at home, keeping them up at night.

Good luck, and enjoy the journey!

www.ingramcontent.com/pod-product-compliance
Lightning Source LLC
Chambersburg PA
CBHW021127080526
44587CB00012B/1160